War Stories

Reporting in the Time of Conflict
From the Crimea to Iraq

This book is based on the "War Stories" exhibit created by the Newseum, for which Harold Evans served as guest curator. Additional writing was done by Donald Ross, Senior Editor of the Newseum. "War Stories" uses vignettes from journalists past and present and examines war reporting from the mid-19th century to the present. It documents the emergence of the independent war correspondent and the issues that confront those who report conflict.

The Newseum is the world's only interactive museum of news. It will have a new home, at 555 Pennsylvania Avenue in Washington, D.C., in 2006.

War Stories

Reporting in the Time of Conflict
From the Crimea to Iraq

HAROLD EVANS

BUNKER HILL PUBLISHING

BOSTON • LONDON

First published in 2003 by Bunker Hill Publishing Inc.
26 Adams Street, Charlestown, MA 02129 USA
6 The Colonnade, Rye Road, Hawkhurst, Kent TN18 4ES UK

10 9 8 7 6 5 4 3 2 1

Library of Congress Cataloging in Publication Data available from the publisher's office

ISBN 1 59373 005 5

Printed in China by Jade Productions

Contents

Introduction

For journalists, war has always been the most urgent of stories. Human fate and the fortunes of nations hang in the balance.

War reporting often is portrayed as romantic adventure. It may be, but more often it is dirty and depressing—the toughest and most dangerous of assignments. So why are journalists drawn to the chaos of combat? The reasons are many and complex, ranging from idealism to a quest for professional glory. But mostly the allure is simple: war is the biggest story of all.

Today, covering wars presents unprecedented challenges. The sheer number of news outlets has led to new, more intense competition among reporters. While technology makes it possible to file real-time reports from a war zone, it also has spawned an insatiable 24/7 news cycle that ceaselessly demands more and newer material. And reporters struggle with the constant conflict between the public's need to know and the military's need to keep things secret.

Richard Harding Davis cleans his rifle at training camp in Plattsburgh, N.Y., in 1915.

Working as a war correspondent is probably more dangerous than ever. In addition to the usual hazards of combat, today's combatants sometimes target journalists. The Freedom Forum Journalists Memorial bears grim testimony to that hard truth: it carries the names of more than 700 journalists who have died covering wars. Yet when conflict comes, journalists are willing to risk all, as they strive to keep truth from becoming war's first casualty.

War Stories is the first volume in a series of Newseum-produced books about journalism's influence on our lives, from covering wars to watching political campaigns. In *War Stories*, renowned author and editor Harold Evans blends anecdotes and commentary to create a fascinating look at how war has been reported, from Caesar's time to the present. We hope you find it interesting and insightful.

Peter Prichard
President
Freedom Forum

The blood-covered camera of an injured photographer lies on the floor of Baghdad's Palestine Hotel in April 2003. Two journalists were killed and two others were wounded when the hotel was shelled by U.S. forces, who said they were under sniper fire and saw what could have been binoculars in a hotel window. Nine journalists died covering the war in Iraq.

Foreword – The Price of News

When I was asked to be the guest curator of the Newseum exhibition on war correspondents, my immediate image was of a lanky young man standing on the Golan Heights in his shirt sleeves, with an open notebook, interviewing Israeli Gen. Ariel Sharon. David Blundy was the epitome of the modern war correspondent, flung into a series of dangerous missions by the exigencies of news. I was his editor, and I often asked him, and others, to report war. I was the editor of *The Sunday Times* of London, and then of *The Times*, from 1967 to 1982, an era opened by the Six Day War in Israel and closed by Britain's war with Argentina for the Falkland Islands, with much bloodshed in between. At any time, our reporters and photographers were at risk in Vietnam, Cambodia, Northern Ireland, Lebanon, Egypt, Syria and Israel, Biafra, Uganda, Nicaragua and El Salvador, and Ethiopia. In all my years editing in Britain, and again as an editor in America in a later decade, I never met a single hesitation, still less a refusal. On the contrary, the problem was to select from among volunteers and to restrain them from undue risk. I recall giving the instructions, to no avail, that

David Blundy interviews Israel's Ariel Sharon, above, during the Yom Kippur War in 1973. At right, in Egypt.

reporter Jon Swain should be pulled out of Phnom Penh as the murderous Khmer Rouge reached the doomed city, and that photographer Don McCullin no longer be allowed into war zones because he was taking too many chances. They made up their own minds. Editors or no, they did what they felt they had to do.

I thought of David Blundy first because his green backpack, holding barely a razor and a change of shirt, was a metaphor for the approach of the best of them. He did not pack any ready-made conclusions. He did not recklessly expose himself to danger, but he never ceased to expose himself to doubt. This is a risk some of us go to great lengths to avoid. There is comfort in certainty. In journalism, it is simpler to sound off than it is to find out. If Blundy did not quite reach a conclusion on his hazardous forays, he would bring it back like contraband – unwritten, undeclared – until he could put it to the test on a second or third visit. He would hang his long frame over his portable typewriter for so long at such ungodly hours, scowling gloomily into his notebook. "Do you find a problem," he would say, "of getting the words in the right order? What's it all about?"

Writing may be hard for everyone, but it is hardest of all for the war correspondent.

He or she has to find the order of words that neither sensationalize nor downplay, that neither oversimplify nor stupefy, conscious always that lives may be at stake, that decisions of gravity may be taken on the strength of a few hundred words. Is the story accurate? Is it clear? Is it fair? How much personal emotion should it contain, if any? Is it meaningful? David, naturally, doubted whether he met the tests he set himself. On assignment from Britain's *The Correspondent* in El Salvador's civil war on Nov. 17, 1989, he already had filed a good dispatch. Then he called in that morning to say he was going out in the barrio to see if he should top up the story with one last paragraph. There, on a street corner, a random bullet took his young life.

It seemed to those of us who were his friends that his "last paragraph" was a mortal redundancy. And yet the unwritten last paragraph, the untaken last photo frame, is the true memorial of the war correspondent. To Blundy, there was a chance that the material gathered for his last paragraph just might affect the balance and readability of his story, and that was all that mattered. Another of my reporters, Nick Tomalin, also was on the Golan Heights in the same mood. He did not come back, either. He and the hundreds of war correspondents who have died in the line of duty give what we call freedom of the press its moral energy.

Cameraman Paul Moran died in the war in Iraq in 2003 very much as David Blundy died in El Salvador. He was trying to do his job the very best way he could. Moran was seeking the perfect image for the Australian Broadcasting Corporation as Blundy sought the perfect story. Moran was filming near a chaotic checkpoint leading into the village of Khormal, near the town of Halabja in the remote corner of northern Iraq where the Kurds and U.S. forces were flushing out Ansar al-Islam, a terrorist group linked to the 9/11 al-Qaeda. Something caused the Kurdish militia to run in panic from the checkpoint. Moran didn't run. He kept walking toward the checkpoint, filming. A white taxi drove toward him. Its driver signaled to Moran to move closer. When he did, the car stopped beside him and then exploded. The suicide bomber and Moran died instantly; two Kurds died, and another ABC correspondent, Eric Campbell, was injured.

There was no need for Moran to walk toward his death. There was no need for Michael Kelly to be in Iraq at all in April 2003. He reported the Gulf War of 1991 and wrote a fine book about it called "Martyrs' Day." This time he was happily ensconced as editor of *The Atlantic* and a syndicated columnist for *The Washington Post*, but he was convinced the war was right and he wanted to endorse his conviction with his physical presence. He paid for that with his life.

Michael, distinctive in life, was distinguished in death. He was the first "embedded" journalist to die in the war. Some 600 reporters, print and television, were embedded, meaning they had accepted the Pentagon's invitation to be assigned to specific combat units instead of hanging around at a rearward base waiting for briefings by commanders, as in the first Gulf War, or adventuring more or less on their own, as in Vietnam. In Iraq, they exchanged unique access for the privilege of getting shot at. Michael was apparently traveling with soldiers in a Humvee military vehicle which attracted gunfire. The driver swerved off the road, and they plunged into a canal. NBC's boyish David Bloom did not have to be in Iraq either. He was already renowned as an anchorman but chose to go. He fitted up a special vehicle, the "Bloom-mobile," for his embedded video transmissions. It was a shock to see him one day talking to us cheerfully from atop a tank rolling along a road outside Baghdad, sending amazingly clear pictures, and the next to hear that he was dead at 39, stricken by a pulmonary

11

embolism, perhaps attributable to the hours of cramped privation.

At least a dozen journalists died covering the war. Considering the ratio of deaths to participants, being a correspondent in Iraq was far more dangerous than being there as part of the military. Curiously, most of the correspondents who died were not embedded. Two reporters, one for Reuters, Taras Protsyuk, and one from Spanish television, Jose Couso, were in a Baghdad hotel packed with international journalists. They were killed when a U.S. tank fired on the hotel in response, it was said, to sniper fire. The reporters in the building denied any fire had come from there; accusations proliferated that the U.S. military had deliberately set out to kill reporters. "The U.S. is now murdering journalists," proclaimed Mexico's *El Universal* daily on its front page. The death in a U.S. bombing raid of Tareq Ayyoub, a reporter-producer for Al-Jazeera television network, provoked the Arab media to accuse the United States of intentionally "killing witnesses." That was paranoid; precision bombing is not that precise. The fatalities were the tragic accidents of war, no more deliberate than the deaths of nearly fifty military men killed by their own side by "friendly fire" in the heat of battle. The only journalist targeted for being a journalist was Moran. He was apparently singled out and deliberately targeted.

Embedding was widely considered a brilliant success. The Pentagon got reporters who identified with the military. The press got its story. The embeddeds could not give the broader perspective on the progress of the war, but the reporters in print and television certainly excelled in giving us the sense of battle; it would have been even more spectacular if the networks and cable stations had felt able to pool their images. In any event, nobody at home has ever seen combat that close up and as it happened. It was surreal to be a viewer – opining in comfort and flinching from the bullets. Television itself, in fact, did not seem quite to realize what treasure it had, all too often cutting away to studio bromides. I would guess that the American public has never held its fighting men in higher esteem. The demeanor of the men under extreme stress was impressive and that was vividly conveyed by newspapers, radio and television.

Censorship has never been less onerous. The embedded reporters had to accept certain ground rules, most importantly that they not reveal details – locations in particular – that would frustrate the war planners and endanger troops. Since to do so would also endanger the reporter, it was readily honored by the press, with only two exceptions among the very many thousands of reports. Geraldo Rivera, the maverick television showman criticized for carrying a gun on assignment in Afghanistan, sketched a map in the sand for Fox News. The Pentagon maintained it could show the enemy the whereabouts of the U.S. Army's 101st Airborne Division and where troops might advance next. Philip Smucker, a freelancer for *The Christian Science Monitor,* was similarly accused of revealing a Marine position during a CNN interview. The Pentagon, reasonably enough, expelled both men from Iraq. Fox News, which reported the war throughout on a high note of patriotism, was surprisingly tolerant of Rivera's lapse. He made up for it by staging a presentation to the world of the 4th Infantry Division (Mechanized) in Kuwait, which was a quite moving moment with men about to go into harm's way.

More intriguing questions are raised in the embedding experiment. In the approaches to Baghdad, a reporter on top of a tank filmed an Iraqi soldier by the side of the road on his knees. Someone shouted to him to put his haversack aside. As he did, another man came through the trees behind him. The reporter yelled to the tank crew, "Don't shoot!" The advancing man was indeed unarmed, and the crew did not shoot. The humanitarian instinct was admirable – but was it not a breach of the canons of journalism? How would the reporter and the soldiers with him have felt if the man had had a concealed weapon and contrived to shoot one of them, or explode himself as a suicide bomber? And what is an embedded correspondent to do if someone next to him is bleeding to death? Keep taking notes? Start up the satellite video link?

In another memorable video, when U.S. soldiers were pinned down in a long firefight at an underpass, the question was raised on air whether the reporter, too, should pick up a gun and return fire. Most people would understand if he did, in a life or death situation, but it is well to recognize the implications when objectivity is sacrificed. The crude hysterical jingoism originating mainly in the studios after many hours of cable news of the Iraqi war was a disservice to the simple valor of men in the field, to say nothing of one's credibility as news purveyor. I happened to be a supporter of the invasion (and a critic of the premature ending in 1991), but I found it demeaning for blowhard anchors to vent about the "sickening treason" of those who had exercised their right to criticize; after all, the operation was called "Iraqi Freedom." CNN, as a genuinely

13

NBC News correspondent David Bloom covered the war in Iraq from a self-contained news vehicle that he helped design. Bloom, 39, who slept in the "Bloom-mobile" – actually a tank recovery vehicle – died of an embolism thought to have been caused by cramped conditions in the vehicle.

international news service, was the only one of the three cable-news networks that refrained from using the flag as a logo. Wrapping everything in a flag is too easy. It is cheap marketing and it is bound to raise the suspicion that unpalatable truths will be glossed over. The value of being able to believe what we hear, what we read, is incalculable.

It was sad that the legendary Peter Arnett was fired from NBC for the ill-judged sycophancy of his reporting from Baghdad. CNN, in the postwar, was accused of giving up the truth for access when its chief news executive, Eason Jordan, revealed that the channel had withheld reports of Saddam Hussein's atrocities. Jordan is an honorable man who had intended his article in *The New York Times* as an example of the ambiguities of decision-making. The network knew that one of CNN's Iraqi cameramen had been tortured and it knew that Hussein's son Uday was threatening the lives of King Hussein of Jordan and two of Uday's brothers-in-law, then in exile. CNN privately warned the king, but it sat on the other news for fear of betraying its sources in Iraq. The brothers-in-law went back to their deaths. Protecting the life of a source is a very good reason for restraint, but CNN would have been better advised to remove its bureau and its associates, and then publish what it knew. Preserving its bureau at some cost to its reputation was a loss. The Arab world, in particular, where CNN is popular, deserved every bit of evidence on how evil the regime was. (The historical playoff between access and truth is discussed later in this book.)

There is a very practical reason for working journalists to honor the Geneva

Convention that insists upon reporters staying out of the fighting. It protects them and it protects the ability to report conflict at all. Journalists are afforded the same protection as civilians "provided they take no action adversely affecting their status." When war correspondents become warriors they risk not only their own lives and the lives of their colleagues but the very institution they serve. The issue was raised obliquely when CNN's Brent Sadler, an experienced reporter, and his camera crew drove into the city of Tikrit ahead of U.S. troops. Gunmen pulled alongside them. Sadler and his men were traveling with armed security. After an exchange of gunfire the CNN crew escaped. So far, so good. But did they compromise their journalistic status? Did they compromise it any more than an embedded journalist traveling with the armed security of the U.S. Army? *The Wall Street Journal* thinks they did: "CNN repeatedly aired footage of the incident which certainly made for dramatic TV. But our concern is that it also sent a message that all journalists are potential combatants and that they all travel with security who are armed. . . . Just as firing from ambulances would endanger all medics, a repeat of Mr. Sadler's armed rush to Tikrit would put all journalists in harm's way." There is force in this argument. The dilemma is that in many areas of conflict a clearly identified unarmed journalist is at risk from people who have never heard of the Geneva Convention and wouldn't care if they had. The abduction and murder of Daniel Pearl in Pakistan testifies to that, as do numerous deaths in Afghanistan. In the end, the price for finding out may be just unbearable.

What follows is a glimpse of the rich variety of characters who have gone to battle with a pen or camera, and the complications of their calling. In their long history – for wars have always been with us – there is much romance and adventure, but a brutal reality, too. And there are many questions. Should a correspondent or the editor ever put truth second to his own country's perceived national interests? What does history have to tell us about the consequences of evading the censor? In foreign wars, is it ever proper to sympathize with one side or another? Should a correspondent always keep a professional detachment or has he or she a higher duty when it is possible to intervene and save a life? What public benefit is there – if any – in the firsthand picture of conflict, or does it amount to no more than voyeurism? There are no simple answers.

Harold Evans
New York, April 2003

The War Correspondent

History turned on the success of the invasion, but the scene on the beach was desperate. The ships could not get close enough to put the soldiers ashore. Hands full and weighed down by the heavy burden of their arms, the soldiers had to simultaneously jump from the ships, get a footing in chest-deep waves, and fight the enemy, who, standing unencumbered on dry and familiar ground, could so easily kill and maim the invaders.

The war correspondent reporting the scene in those terms observed: "These perils frightened our soldiers, who were quite unaccustomed to battles of this kind, with the result that they did not show the same alacrity and enthusiasm as they usually did on dry land."

The candor may strike an odd note. In the mythology of war, our men are never beset by elemental fear, still less paralyzed by it. The lexicon of defeat, if it has to be admitted, is of gallant retreats against over-

Robert Capa, struggling in the waves himself, shot this dramatic photograph of the landing at Omaha Beach. It is one of just a handful of his D-Day photos that survived a darkroom accident.

17

whelming odds. But the war correspondent writing the story of the battle on that beach was uninhibited. He faced none of the frustrations and dilemmas of the modern war correspondent because he was taking part in the battle himself, as the commanding general of the invasion of Britain in the year 55 B.C.

Julius Caesar is one of a very long line of soldiers who reported their own campaigns firsthand. Thucydides was a military officer, and his "History of the Peloponnesian War" was informed by his experience in command of the Greek fleet at Thasos in 424 B.C. and his defeat by the Spartan general Brasidas. The professional independent war correspondent, the unarmed civilian whose pen is supposed to be mightier than the sword, does not arrive on the scene until the Crimean War (1853-55) in the persons of William "Billy" Howard Russell of *The Times* of London, Edwin Lawrence Godkin of the *London Daily News* and G.L. Gruneisen of the *Morning Post*. So it is as well to acknowledge that our perennial appetite for news of war has been served by "amateurs" from time immemorial, in oral history, in poem and song, in legend and myth, in drawing and painting and tapestry.

We know how English axmen cut down the Norman armored knights at the Battle of Hastings in 1066, and how King Harold died on Senlac Hill with an arrow in his eye, because it is all recorded on the Bayeux Tapestry. Mark Kellogg, a Western freelance newspaper reporter, set out to tell us what happened on the morning of June 26, 1876, on a hill at Little Bighorn in Montana. "By the time this reaches you we will have met and fought the red

The drawings of Red Horse, based on tribal lore, provide a sense of the Battle of the Little Bighorn. Only the Indians present knew what actually occurred at the 1876 battle.

devils with what result remains to be seen," he wrote from Rosebud Creek the day before. "I go with [Lt. Col. George] Custer and will be at the death." And indeed he did die with the dashing officer who had disobeyed orders and allowed the reporter to ride along with the 7th Cavalry. Our idea of how every man with Custer perished comes from individual oral accounts retold by Sioux and Cheyenne warriors, father to son and grandson, vividly supplemented by 41 pictographs drawn by Red Horse, a Mıniconjou Lakota chief at the battle. Only in 1999 were all the elements of this war story properly compiled in book form by Herman J. Viola ("Little Bighorn Remembered").

Whoever is the chronicler, there is an eternal and compelling curiosity about war, about wars in which our own survival is at stake, and wars long past. So much heroism; so much folly; so many brilliant moves; so many blunders; so many might-have-beens. In a current conflict, we fret about loved ones; but in all war reports we share vicariously in the terrible excitement of combat. We exult in victories; but we want to know whether the cause is just, the means proportionate to the end, and the execution honorable. We relish the drama of the front line, but we expect to be advised if a decent patriotism is being exploited. Do the

Close-Up

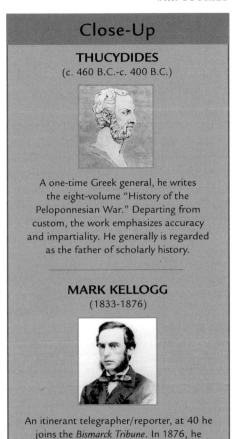

THUCYDIDES
(c. 460 B.C.-c. 400 B.C.)

A one-time Greek general, he writes the eight-volume "History of the Peloponnesian War." Departing from custom, the work emphasizes accuracy and impartiality. He generally is regarded as the father of scholarly history.

MARK KELLOGG
(1833-1876)

An itinerant telegrapher/reporter, at 40 he joins the *Bismarck Tribune*. In 1876, he accompanies Lt. Col. George Custer's campaign against allied Indian tribes. He dies with Custer's command in the Battle of the Little Bighorn.

Viet Cong represent a nationalist rebellion or aggression by international communism? Are there really vital national interests in sending 500,000 U.S. troops into battle to eject Iraq from Kuwait? And the arguments go on long after the battlefield has been cleared of its dead.

For the modern war correspondent, the imponderables are more numerous and the canvas broader than it was for battle participants like Caesar, who practiced war journalism before it was invented. The soldier-reporters were more exposed to risk than the professional correspondent, but in reporting they had a simpler task. They had access, by definition. They were their own censors. They had no worry that their messages and histories would inadvertently cost lives because communication was so slow and restricted. They could take their time in reporting; they had no competition and their eyewitness accounts were idiosyncratic.

Nobody could match Capt. Robert Blakeney's account of the battle of Nivelle in 1813, when the French were finally driven out of Spain. Rushing an enemy redoubt at the head of his regiment, his sword raised, he was struck by a shot that shattered two bones of his left leg. The regiment went on without him, but lying unmolested among the dead and the dying he had a unique view of the battlefield:

The awful events passing lay beneath my view; nor was there aught to interrupt my observation save a few bodily twitches, the pangs of prostrated ambition, and the shot and shells which burst close, or nearly cut the ground from under me.

In my view, the birth and maturation of the unarmed professional war correspondent had four midwives: Democracy. Time. Scale. Speed.

Democracy, nurtured by nearly universal suffrage and popular education, meant governments had more and more to justify the blood, tears, toil and sweat of going to war. And the advent of total war widened the risks beyond the fighting men to every man, woman and child in the nation. Newspapers naturally played on the notion that only independent reporting would satisfy the popular appetite. The fact that war stories sold more newspapers than anything else only demonstrates that high-mindedness and commercial gain are not always in conflict. Governments, for their part, became willing to provide battlefield access for reporters because they presumed the journalists would wave the flag.

Timeliness was the second midwife, first recognized by *The Times* in London. The newspaper abandoned the traditional practice of relying on letters from junior officers at the battlefront when its readers clamored to know what was happening day by day in the Crimean peninsula, where England, with France and the Ottoman Turks, was fighting the Russians. Lt. Charles Naysmith of the East India Company's Bombay Artillery was covering the fighting for *The Times,* but he was thought to have no sense of urgency; perhaps his first priority was staying alive. The frustrated *Times* manager rebuked the foreign editor: "I wish you would impress upon Naysmith with all your eloquence the absolute necessity of writing as often as he can and sending letters without delay." The letters took more than week to arrive anyway, coming by horse and steamer. The appointment of a stocky Irishman, William Howard Russell, was the trailblazing result, and the term "war correspondent" was apt, for the editor of *The Times,* John Delane, asked Russell to write him letters. Delane decided what he would take from them, for use in his news and opinion columns. When Russell saw the scandals in the Crimea, he asked, "Am I to tell these things or hold my tongue?" Delane urged Russell to report all he saw, then withheld from publication any material he deemed

too sensitive. But the information he kept from the public he made certain to circulate among government ministers.

Above, William Howard Russell outfitted to cover the Crimean War. Foreground, his notebook.

Inside Story

MURROW SETS THE TONE FOR ON-THE-SCENE REPORTING

In the mid-19th century, reports from the Crimean War take two weeks or more to reach London. Over time, technology eliminates that lapse. In the Civil War, the telegraph allows newspapers to report a battle just a day or two later.

Radio makes live, on-the-scene reporting possible. In World War II, Edward R. Murrow's CBS broadcasts are the benchmark. He brings the Battle of Britain directly into American homes from London rooftops. His vivid descriptions are interspersed with the sounds of sirens and bombs.

Murrow later moves to television, which adds a new dimension to war reporting. In the late

Edward R. Murrow

1960s, images of Vietnam are such a staple of evening newscasts, that an author dubs the conflict the "living room war."

The fax machine enhances the telephone, a reporting tool that predates World War II. By the 1990s laptop computers and portable satellite uplinks are appearing. Today, technology allows news reports to be transmitted instantly from almost anywhere.

The third midwife was **Scale.** Bigger, longer and more far-flung wars required more trained observers, more coordination of their efforts.

Speed. Finally, communication speeded up and with it competition between publishers and editors to have reporters cunning in the means of transmission and the evasion of bureaucracy. Curiously, in the 21st century communication is so transformed that we are at the dawn of a new era where the war correspondent yields ground to the ordinary citizen. Today, people may speak directly to others by e-mail and the Internet, reporting their own experiences – unfiltered by journalist, editor or censor.

During the 1999 Kosovo war, a Web site organized by The Institute for War and Peace Reporting (www.iwpr.net) attracted contributions from ordinary citizens. One described what it was like to be caught up in ethnic cleansing in Pristina:

> *Armed men wearing black masks and blue police helmets just came and said, "You have to leave." I watched the people flee from their homes through my window. They left all their possessions behind – they weren't even allowed to take their identification cards. All they had was the sadness in their eyes.*

Later, when Kosovo was occupied by NATO, the same nonpartisan Web site was open to Serbs reporting attacks on them by returning Kosovars. Web-site and e-mail reports like this will enrich the coverage of war, but they have the weakness of their openness: They can easily be manipulated. I don't believe they will ever supplant the professional correspondent and the authority of a recognized news organization in the way the reporter supplanted the literate soldier.

The real explosion of professional coverage came with the U.S. Civil War. As in all things, America went in for mass production. Newspapers in the South still relied heavily on telegrams and letters from serving officers, but at least 500 reporters covered the war for the North – after a fashion. In the summary of Phillip Knightley, author of the seminal history of war reporting, "The First Casualty," the adjectives that could be pinned on the reporters' chests were ignorant, dishonest, unethical, inaccurate, partisan and inflammatory.

The nonprofessionals had a better record than that. In the Napoleonic Wars, brilliant firsthand accounts of the battles of Trafalgar and Waterloo come to us from soldiers and sailors. Caesar had as good an eye for a story as any tabloid reporter. This is

Martha Gellhorn with Allied troops at Cassino, Italy, in 1944.

23

how he related what happened to the Roman legionnaires skulking in their ships rather than face the Anglo-Saxon javelins:

> The man who carried the eagle of the tenth legion, after praying to the gods that his action might bring good luck to the legion, cried in a loud voice, "Jump down, comrades, unless you want to surrender our eagle to the enemy; I, at any rate, mean to do my duty to my country and my general." With these words he leapt out of the ship and advanced toward the enemy with the eagle in his hands. At this the soldiers, exhorting each other not to submit to such a disgrace, jumped with one accord from the ship, and the men from the next ships, when they saw them, followed them and advanced against the enemy.

Caesar's report is eerily reminiscent of the scene at Omaha Beach on D-Day when the men of the 1st Division and 29th Division, supported by the 2nd Ranger Battalion, tried to get ashore. Men carrying 66 pounds of equipment had to jump into water that not only was deep but laced with booby traps and mines; many drowned. Those who made it to the beach – mostly to the wrong sectors, for which they had not been trained – curled up in the sand behind the seawall, pinned down by intense machine-gun, rifle, mortar and artillery fire from the sheer cliffs above. Gen. Omar Bradley's beachhead, like Caesar's, would have been lost but for inspired leadership – in a richer idiom. "Get the hell off this damn beach and go kill some Germans," screamed Col. Charles Canham at an officer taking refuge in a pillbox. "Get your ass out of there and show some leadership." Col. George Taylor famously yelled, "Two kinds of people are staying on this beach: the dead and those who are going to die. Now let's get the hell out of here."

We owe these scenes to postwar writers who have made an attempt to reconstruct Omaha Beach. At the time, the reality of the landing, its full horror, its blunders and the awesome nature of its heroism did not come through. There were 558 accredited print and radio correspondents for the five Normandy landings, but the arena was vast and chaotic. They were restricted by censorship as well as by German soldiers doing their damnedest to nail anything that moved. Censors went on the beaches with the reporters, checking that none of them wrote or radioed dispatches that would help the enemy or dismay people at home.

The correspondents filed 700,000 words on the first day. Ernie Pyle, arriving on the second day, sent three dispatches from Omaha Beach, and Martha Gellhorn reported from one of the hospital ships after getting ashore as a stretcher-bearer. Radio transmitted into living rooms the sound of gunfire and men's cheers and ship's whistles and planes. The reports were all very exciting, but readers and listeners were not encouraged to imagine men in a funk, or told that infantry were landing with weapons inferior to the Germans' in every category, except artillery, or that the U.S. Navy launched assault craft so far out that most of the amphibious tanks and guns were swamped and sank in heavy seas, or that among the 2,500 Americans dead at the end of the first day were 40 percent of the combat engineers. The much-loved Pyle, who footslogged with the grunts in North Africa, Sicily, Italy, France and the Pacific, was laconic: "Our men were pinned down for a while, but finally they stood up and went through, and so we took that beach and accomplished our landing."

The cryptic reticence is explicable, but the consequence of the way the landing was covered at the time was well summed up by Max Hastings in his 1984 reconstruction of D-Day ("Overlord: D-Day and the Battle for Normandy"): "Few Europeans and Americans of the postwar generation have grasped just how intense were the early Overlord battles." The folk memory is of an effort of fearless superiority. Steven Spielberg's epic film "Saving Private Ryan" has finally done something to redress this notion. The film is a work of singular imagination. Spielberg was not even born when the Americans went ashore. He does not attempt to suggest what went wrong. His portrayal of the landings is impressionistic, but it is a masterpiece of cinematic art. It

Ernie Pyle, as usual at the center of a cluster of enlisted men; this time it's a tank crew at Anzio, Italy.

25

An undated, signed portrait of Stephen Crane made in Athens, Greece, and inscribed to the managing editor of the New York Journal, *Sam S. Chamberlain.*

evokes the ordeal of the men on the beach; it makes their achievement all the more memorable. "Saving Private Ryan" is very like Stephen Crane's "The Red Badge of Courage." Crane had not seen military action anywhere when he published his novel in 1895. Spielberg was unconcerned with the larger picture or the logistics, with the essential pith of war reporting, and Crane was unconcerned with Stonewall Jackson's tactics in the woods at Chancellorsville where his soldier-coward had his epiphany.

But works of such artistic imagination give us a sense of the emotions and chaos of the battlefield. And there are many: Virginia Cowles in the middle of the panic-stricken flight from Paris in June

1940; John Hersey in the jungle on Guadalcanal in 1942; Tom Wolfe on the aircraft carrier Coral Sea in 1967, recreating life-and-death minutes in the day of a Navy pilot on missions over North Vietnam; Michael Herr a year later evoking the spirit of the besieged Marines at Khe Sanh. They are answers to the questions Walt Whitman posed so poetically:

> *What history, I say, can ever give – for who can know – the mad, determin'd tussle of the armies, in all their separate large and small squads – as this – each steep'd from crown to toe in desperate, mortal purports? Who know the conflict, hand-to-hand – the many conflicts in the dark, those shadowy-tangled, flashing moon beam'd woods – the writhing groups and squads – the cries, the din, the cracking guns and pistols – the distant cannon – the cheers and calls and threats and awful music of the oaths – the indescribable mix – the officers' orders, persuasions, encouragements – the devils fully roused in human hearts – the strong shout, Charge, men charge – the flash of naked sword, and rolling flame and smoke?*

Who are the writers and photographers and artists who have dared to answer Whitman's cry, risking all in the cannon's mouth for the elusive words or pictures that in the wild dark might light up a fragment of truth?

THE WAR CORRESPONDENT

Today it's not 'conventional war reporting'

Tom Gjelten, *National Public Radio*

Tom Gjelten spent eight years on overseas assignments for National Public Radio from 1986 to 1994. During that time he covered conflict in Central America, the Persian Gulf, Croatia and Bosnia. He reports on international issues for NPR.

Tom Gjelten in Bosnia.

"These days . . . it's not a conventional war-reporting situation, where you're maybe embedded with the military forces of the country from which you come and to which you are reporting.

"Wars today are fought with many armed groups. And this is to an extent true in all the conflicts we face in this world. There are paramilitary groups. There are armed civilians. There are government forces. There are organized rebel armies. There are peacekeeping forces. Sometimes there are outside armies – whether from NATO or from a neighboring state – that become involved.

"So it's not just a question of what the military will allow you to do. It's dealing with a whole range of military, paramilitary, various kinds of armed groups, some of which are highly disciplined and make it clear to you right from the beginning what you can do and what you can expect from them.

"Others are very chaotic, undisciplined, lawless, in which you think you have an arrangement with one commander, then all of a sudden you find yourself in a situation where the arrangement you thought you had doesn't exist; where there don't seem to be any rules; where there doesn't seem to be any regulation. Those are, of course, much more dangerous, and much more difficult circumstances for a journalist."

Romance
vs. Reality

The war correspondent trails clouds of glory. The names of the pioneers of the trade are stardust: Ernest Hemingway, Alexander Dumas, Henry Villard, Winston Churchill, Stephen Crane, John Reed, Arthur Conan Doyle, Rudyard Kipling, Richard Harding Davis, John Dos Passos, John Steinbeck, Jack London, George Orwell, Philip Gibbs, Luigi Barzini. The names from World War II, Korea and Vietnam, the Gulf War and Kosovo are likewise as redolent of adventure and derring-do, with photojournalists, and radio and television commentators crowding the pantheon.

They are the eyes of history – when they are allowed to be.

William Howard Russell is with the British command on a plateau overlooking Balaklava on Oct. 25, 1854, watching in horrified fascination as the 600-plus proud men of the elite Light Brigade misunderstand a command and charge straight into the Russian guns.

Lt. Barrett Gallagher, a photographer with Edward Steichen's Naval Aviation Photographic Unit, aboard a carrier-borne warplane in 1945.

Close-Up

LOWELL THOMAS
(1892-1981)

A baritone-voiced globetrotter, he is a pioneering news broadcaster whose voice is recognized by millions. Also known as newsreel narrator and prolific author, in World War I he immortalizes British officer T.E. Lawrence – "Lawrence of Arabia."

VIRGINIA IRWIN
(1908-1980)

Arriving in France after D-Day, Irwin accompanies U.S. forces through Europe. But her greatest scoop – an unauthorized visit to besieged Berlin – languishes on a censor's desk, held up because of her infraction of Army rules.

Nearly half are killed, wounded or captured.

Archibald Forbes steels his nerves inside the British square at Ulunidi, Natal, as it braces to resist thousands of onrushing Zulu warriors in 1879, then rides 300 miles in 50 hours with his scoop.

In the Boxer Rebellion in 1900, **Luigi Barzini** stands with 100 Cossacks confronted by 2,000 saber-wielding rebels determined to slice them to pieces.

Thomas Morris Chester, the son of a former slave, sits in the speaker's chair in the Confederate leglislature in 1865 to write a dispatch that at last will do justice to the valor of the black troops who were among the first to enter Richmond.

Sylvanus Cadwallader is in the McLean house in Virginia when Union officers squabble over souvenirs after Robert E. Lee's surrender to Ulysses S. Grant in 1865.

Lowell Thomas meets Col. T.E. Lawrence in the desert fighting the Turks in World War I and creates Lawrence of Arabia.

At Guernica in the Spanish Civil War, **Noel Monks** and **George L. Steer** are near enough to testify that it was Nationalist squadrons of German warplanes that dropped incendiaries and high explosives and machine-gunned civilians.

The war artist **Tom Lea** crawls with the Marines under Japanese mortar and rifle fire on Pelelieu Island; **Bill Mauldin** draws his popular cartoon, "Hit th' dirt, boys!" after he is "nicked" by mortar fire "sliding down one of those mountains in Italy."

Virginia Irwin and **Andrew Tully** ride with Soviet forward troops to see the final bloodletting in Berlin in 1945.

Jon Swain, **Sidney Schanberg** and **Alan Rockoff** risk their lives in May 1975 to stay in Phnom Penh for the arrival of the murderous Khmer Rouge, and witness the cruel mass expulsions into the Killing Fields.

And then there are the photographers. George Rodgers at Bergen-Belsen and Margaret Bourke-White at Buchenwald incontrovertibly document the evil of the Holocaust. In the Korean War, David Douglas Duncan immortalizes the stoicism of the Marines on the long icy retreat from Chosin Reservoir. Giles Peress captures the moments when civilians died under fire on Bloody Sunday in Northern Ireland.

Television's moving pictures have their own velocity, but they clearly have not supplanted the still photograph, which has more affinity with the way we summon images to mind. Who cannot recall the image first published in the French magazine *Vu* in September 1936 that made Robert Capa instantly famous – the moment of death of a Republican militiaman, flung

Close-Up

BILL MAULDIN
(1921–2002)

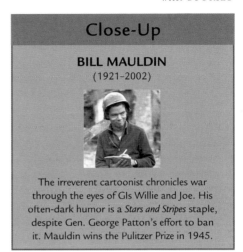

The irreverent cartoonist chronicles war through the eyes of GIs Willie and Joe. His often-dark humor is a *Stars and Stripes* staple, despite Gen. George Patton's effort to ban it. Mauldin wins the Pulitzer Prize in 1945.

backwards by a bullet, his rifle arm outstretched as he falls on a scrubby hillside?

Three still pictures by war photographers stay in our minds as symbols of Vietnam: Malcolm Browne's 1963 photograph of a monk's fiery death; Eddie Adams' 1968 image of an officer shooting a prisoner in the head on a Saigon street during Tet; Nick Ut's 1972 photograph of a naked 9-year-old Vietnamese girl running toward the camera from a napalm bombing by the South Vietnamese air force.

Early photographs had to be viewed as prints or as stereoscopic cards, though they also were the basis for engravings in publications

31

such as *Harper's Weekly*. Still, right from the start, photography made an impression, advancing under the banner that the camera could not lie. Of course, it could. Roger Fenton, who was in a way the father of war photojournalism, took a photo wagon to the Crimean War with the deliberate aim of taking photographs that would boost domestic morale after William Howard Russell's exposure of scandalous conditions. Troops who had lacked food and fuel were now shown at the cookhouse and in new tents, with supplies piled up; soldiers who had almost frozen to death were shown in heavy wool clothing; servants poured wine for reclining officers.

No Civil War photographs captured combat; cameras of the era were unable to freeze movement. The many thousands of Civil War photographs made by hundreds of local photographers were commerce rather than journalism – paid portraits of soldiers for loved ones. Just a handful of photographers, chiefly Mathew Brady, Alexander Gardner, Timothy O'Sullivan, George M.

Roger Fenton's "photographic van," with Marcus Sparling aboard. Transporting bulky photo equipment of the mid-19th century required a vehicle of some size.

Barnard and James F. Gibson, actively engaged in photographing conflict. Their classic battlefield images document an end truth about war – men *in extremis*. "It seems somewhat singular," observed *The New York Times* of Brady's pictures from Antietam, "that the same sun that looked down upon the faces of the slain, blistering them, blotting them out from the bodies all semblance of humanity, and hastening corruption, should have thus caught their features upon canvas, and given them perpetuity for ever." But Brady and Gardner rearranged pictures for romantic or heroic effect. Gardner carried a rifle as a prop, laying it beside a corpse where it would help the photo's composition. In a photograph of a dead Confederate at Rose Woods, Gettysburg, he added a severed hand. His Confederate sharpshooter at Devil's Den, Gettysburg, on July 6, 1863, had been dragged 40 yards by Gardner to make "a sentimental composition." When one officer was absent for a group photograph of Gen. William Sherman's staff, Brady took the absentee's photograph later, pasted it in, and rephotographed the group portrait.

There is no journalistic justification for this kind of manipulation, now made dangerously easy by the advent of computer imaging. Manipulating images devalues the

Inside Story

ADJUSTING THE PICTURE DISTORTS THE VIEW

Photography is in its infancy when Mathew Brady and Alexander Gardner establish their reputations as photographers during the U.S. Civil War.

They think nothing of posing corpses on the battlefield or otherwise manipulating photos. Altered or staged photography has been an issue ever since. Critics say Robert Capa's famous 1936 image of a soldier at the moment of death is staged – a charge never proved. Later, Joe Rosenthal is

Gardner photo of a battlefield.

wrongly accused of staging his photo of the Iwo Jima flag-raising in 1945.

In the 1990s *Time* comes under fire when it is discovered that a cover photograph of murder suspect O.J. Simpson is "enhanced" – giving Simpson a sinister appearance. *Newsweek* later engages in photographic orthodontia to improve the appearance of a cover subject's teeth.

Although most mainstream news organizations now have strict policies against doctoring photos, increasingly sophisticated technology broadens the opportunity for the unscrupulous to disprove the adage that "the camera never lies."

33

unique integrity of the photograph as a document. At the very least, pretense should be acknowledged. In World War I, photographs of troops with bayonets going "over the top," and captioned "advancing under fire as steadily as on parade," were posed pictures taken during training, the negatives altered to mask giveaway details. Access was severely restricted for photographers, but Jane Carmichael's study, "First World War Photographers," suggests there was also a tacit agreement among the military, photographers, propagandists and the press that too much dwelling on the horrific dead would offend contemporary standards of decency. Photographers William Rider-Rider and John Warwick Brooke are all the more distinctive because they were dedicated to authenticity. They provided us with images of the appalling battlefields of Passchendale and Ypres that once seen are never forgotten. Their photographs have become "World War I."

Photography of violence is charged with emotion. Editors at *The New York Times* considered Malcolm Browne's 1963 photograph of a South Vietnamese monk setting himself ablaze too much for their readers. The *Times* also downplayed Ronald Haeberle's confirming documentation of the massacre at My Lai, with one picture on Page 3. It felt it had to "balance" this single image with a picture of a child killed by Viet Cong. Readers complained anyway. Kenneth Jarecke's Gulf War image of the charred skeletal head of an Iraqi in a vehicle hit by a rocket was not seen in the United States at the time because an Associated Press editor in New York took it off the wire. The *London Observer* did publish it and was swamped with protests that it was too ghastly. Admittedly it was shocking, but it was still a photograph that respected the human identity of the dead man. It was not meaningless dismembered flesh. As a newspaper editor I have rejected photographs of carnage that are obscene because they do not improve our understanding of the event. They amount to a macabre voyeurism. British television, for the same reason, did not show film of the mangled heaps of flesh after the Serbs shelled a crowded square in Tuzla in the spring of 1995. In the Iraqi case it seems to me that the amateur and professional censors were still attempting to nurture the romantic illusion of war as a conflict where nobody dies a horrible death. CBS cameraman Jim Helling made the proper point. He was in the photographic pool with Jarecke and took film of the truck and other bodies, but he asked Jarecke for a print of the still "because that's the face of war."

David Turnley's compelling Persian Gulf War photo of a soldier's grief.

No questions of taste justified depriving the public sight of David Turnley's Gulf War photograph of a sergeant in a helicopter weeping beside a body bag he has just discovered contains his best buddy, killed by friendly fire. "The Pentagon did everything it could to manage the images that came out of the war," says Turnley. "I was there to document the reality." His picture almost never saw the light of day. Turnley took it when he managed to dodge his military "minder." It was only by chance that he later found his film had been held up at the censor's desk and argued for its release – an argument validated by the image's triumph as World Press Photo of the Year.

35

> *I would say that the war correspondent gets more drinks, more girls, better pay and greater freedom than the soldier.*
>
> Robert Capa

Richard Harding Davis reports from Cuba for Scribner's *(above) and poses beside his elaborate field tent (opposite).*

Such scoops! Such sensations! Such adventures! Such romance! Such camaraderie, swapping yarns in the bistro in Saigon, the Intercontinental in Amman, the Commodore in Beirut! "I would say that the war correspondent gets more drinks, more girls, better pay and greater freedom than the soldier," says the legendary photographer Robert Capa, and promptly goes in with the first wave at Omaha Beach, taking his expensive Burberry raincoat into the landing craft. He ends World War II in Paris having a passionate affair with Ingrid Bergman.

In the Civil War, William Croffut of the *New York Herald Tribune* reads Byron around campfires of Union soldiers awaiting battle. In Paris, besieged by the Prussians in 1870, *The* (London) *Times'* man floats his messages to London out over the front lines by that French innovation, the hot-air balloon. By carrier pigeon he gets back the front page of *The Times* reduced to microscopic size, which is then enlarged and distributed. Trying to capitalize on his readers' war fever, young William Randolph Hearst instructs a correspondent to rescue the 18-year-old daughter of a Cuban insurgent from a Spanish dungeon in Havana, and he does, disguising her as a sailor. Stephen Crane observes Theodore Roosevelt charge up Kettle Hill in 1898, then saunters off in his

khaki suit and slouch hat and captures a town himself. In 1917, Floyd Gibbons chooses to cross the Atlantic on the liner Laconia in the full knowledge it might attract a German U-boat, and it does, giving him a sensational story. Richard Harding Davis, ribbons on his chest, a brace of pistols in his belt and two pairs of binoculars round his neck, survives five wars unscathed but in World War I finds his fondness for fancy attire carries risks. An eight-year-old passport photo, in which he's wearing the uniform of a West African field officer, convinces the Germans that he is a British spy who should go before a firing squad. After a harrowing night in captivity he is released, unharmed but shaken. While other reporters idle in the bars of El Paso, John Reed slips across the border, and catches up with Pancho Villa's bandit army in Chihuahua, Mexico. He rides into action with Villa and his horseback troop, and makes him an icon. Marguerite Higgins, a steely 24-year-old from Oakland, scoops the world at Dachau and swims away from the bullets of the North Korean invaders of

Ernest Hemingway's World War II press credentials.

Seoul. Francois Sully turns up at besieged Dien Bien Phu in 1954 in perfectly pressed fatigues and goes to bed, amid the pounding of artillery, in navy-blue silk pajamas with white piping, toasting the grimy defenders from a silver hip flask of Courvoisier.

The romance is real enough. Nora Ephron wrote in 1973, "It is impossible to realize how much of Ernest Hemingway still lives in the hearts of men until you spend time with the professional war correspondents." She argued that reporting the war, unlike fighting in it, was about the only classic male endeavor left that provided physical danger and personal risk without public disapproval. "The awful truth is that for correspondents war is not hell. It is fun."

It is possible to find ample quotes to confirm her perception. *Life* photographer Tim Page, who raced into combat areas in Vietnam on a motorbike, badly wounded on three occasions, was then asked to write a book that once and for all would take the glamour out of war. "Jesus!" he said, "Take the glamour out of war! How the hell can you do that? You can't take the glamour out of a tank burning or a helicopter blowing up. It's like trying to take the glamour out of sex. War is good for you." Author Knightley believes most correspondents in most wars have had a romantic sense of their jobs, but that disillusion set in for many as the Vietnam War grew more shocking. Certainly, correspondents began seriously to examine their own ethics – making careers out of human misery – but their sensibilities have hardly discouraged their heirs. Greg Marinovich speaks for a generation of young globe-trotting conflict photographers in saying of his experiences in Croatia in 1991: "I find I liked war. There was a peculiar liberating excitement in taking cover from an artillery barrage in a woodshed that offered no protection at all." Marinovich, with South African Kevin Carter, was one of a group of four war photographers who came to be called the Bang-Bang Club – "we liked the credit" – and then had a problem with the numbers of other young photographers who wanted to join the clique. Anthony Loyd, who has reported seven recent wars, called his 1999 book, "My War Gone By, I Miss It So." He was a British army platoon commander in the Gulf War and Northern Ireland who found peacetime civilian life oppressive and took himself off to the Bosnian killing fields: "I cannot apologize for enjoying it so. I took the freedom and light that fighting offered, feeling truly

earthed with the Bosnian War once more. It was like falling in love again."

Of course, war attracts the adventurers because it is big news, the biggest story most correspondents will ever cover. There always will be a thrill in that. The seasoned Charles Mohr, who told it like it was in Vietnam, said, "You see these things, these terrible things, but in an odd way they are good stories."

But for all the romance, there is a reality, too. Live like a sewer rat in a battle zone. Suffer for years as a hostage, like Terry Anderson in Beirut. Take 40 days and 40 nights of brutal treatment from your jailers, like Bob Simon and his CBS crew, captured on the Iraqi border in the Gulf War. Know that independent reporting incites accusations from your fellow countrymen that you are a liar and traitor. Squarely confront the overarching reality for every battlefield correspondent that luck can – and does – run out. Ian Morrison, age 35, of *The Times* and Christopher Buckley, 45, of London's *Daily Telegraph* came unscathed through reporting World War II and were planning to retire from war reporting when Korea lured them back. Their jeep hit a land mine. Ian Roeh was riding with a general in an Israeli-controlled security zone in Lebanon in 1999 when a roadside cluster mine took his life. Swedish-Argentine cameraman **39**

> *If your pictures aren't good enough, you aren't close enough.*
>
> Robert Capa

Yank *correspondent Hyman Goldberg uses a pistol to debunk an advertising claim that this metal-clad New Testament will stop a bullet.*

Leonardo Henricksen, working for Swedish television, has left us the most telling image of reality: the moment he died. Reporting a coup attempt in Santiago, Chile, in 1973, he aimed his camera at a soldier pointing a rifle at him. The soldier shot him dead.

Capa said, "If your pictures aren't good enough, you aren't close enough," and the mortality rate of photographers is astounding. No fewer than 135 photographers of different nations were killed or disappeared while covering the several wars in Indochina; 45 reporters are known to have died. The debonair Capa was unashamed to admit that in the surf with dead soldiers at Omaha Beach he "had it bad," the camera trembling in his hands, a "new kind of fear shaking my body from toe to hair and twisting my face." Ten years later, on May 25, 1954, he stepped on a land mine in Vietnam. His peer Larry Burrows went down in a helicopter crash. Gilles Caron, the co-founder of the Gamma Agency, was captured by Viet Cong inside Cambodia in 1970 and never seen again.

They were unlucky; some invite death. In the Suez War of 1956, Magnum's David Seymour (also known as Chim), in a borrowed British army uniform, and Jean Roy of *Paris Match,* took a jeep to drive down the

Robert Capa's last photo, from Vietnam in 1954.
Minutes later he stepped on a mine and was killed.

causeway. A cease-fire had been declared, but they were stopped by a British officer and warned not to go beyond his final outpost. They gave him the "V sign" and roared on. The next order was from an Egyptian outpost: Stop. They roared on again, only this time they were machine-gunned.

Press credentials and public position are little protection in the new little hot wars. Egon Scotland of *Suddeutsche Zeitung* was riding in a clearly marked press car in 1991 when shot dead by Serbian militia. Agus Muliawan was traveling with a group of nine church workers on a relief mission for refugees in East Timor in 1999, but Indonesian troops slew them all indiscriminately. Every conflict claims its press victims. Kosovo is thought of as a sanitized affair, an air campaign with mass briefings away from the action, but at least three journalists were among the hundreds of civilian fatalities. In that number was Slavko Curuvijia, the editor and publisher of *Dnevni Telegraph*, who had been critical of Slobodan Milosevic and his government. He was assassinated outside his apartment.

There were 30 or so other wars going on at the same time, with journalists at risk in every one of them. They are taken for granted. Rarely does the murder of a journalist provoke the kind of reaction it did in Nicaragua when Pedro Chamorro, the publisher of *La Prensa*, was gunned down after he had criticized President Anastasio Somoza. It led to a revolution that Somoza had to flee, and eventually the election of Chamorro's widow, Violeta, as president.

War correspondents can rarely point to such a positive result for the risks they take. Some do not even try. Their habit is to affect a devil-may-care attitude about the value of their work. They see themselves as "war junkies," flamboyantly there for the hell of it. I think this is more a rationalization than a true reflection, but there is a rough distinction, historically and today, between the undeniable "cowboys" and those who could be categorized as "believers." Believers tend to be less reckless than the adventurers; they are not in it for the exhilarating scent of danger or the adrenaline rush. They calibrate the risks, trying to recognize the moment when the story becomes secondary to survival. But common to all of them, I find, is a sense of fraternity. Egon Scotland died because he went out searching for an inexperienced colleague who was late coming back from the field. A loss among the brotherhood can invite impulses at once foolish and admirable. In the Nigerian civil war in 1968, CBS reporter Morley Safer braved a hail of machine-gun bullets to retrieve free-lancer Priyan Samrakha who had been shot by a sniper, fatally as it turned out.

Photographer Don McCullin of *The Sunday Times*, a true believer in awakening the public conscience, had been on the front lines over and over again in Cyprus, the Congo, Vietnam, Iran, Afghanistan and Central America. He was wounded in Cambodia and held in Uganda in 1972. Yet a year later, in the Yom Kippur War, McCullin did not hesitate when an Israeli officer on the Golan Heights told him that the car driven into a valley by his colleague Nick Tomalin had been blown up by a Syrian missile. Like a man possessed, McCullin brushed past the restraining Israeli officer and ran into the Syrian-targeted valley of death, willing Tomalin to be alive so that he could carry him back. Tomalin would have done the same. Tomalin was in the classic mold, more a romantic than a believer, but a professional, renowned for a brilliant report from Vietnam ("The General Goes Zapping Charlie Cong," 1966). He was on sabbatical when the Yom Kippur War started, writing a book and, at the moment the news broke, practicing a Mozart clarinet concerto. He insisted on being sent. It might be fun.

ROMANCE vs. REALITY

'Brief moments of terror'

Ted Koppel, *ABC*

Ted Koppel is best known to most television viewers as the host of ABC-TV's "Nightline." But in his 38-year career with ABC, Koppel spent much time as a foreign bureau chief and a diplomatic correspondent, jobs that often found him covering war.

Donatella Lorch, above, in the Persian Gulf. At left, Ted Koppel.

Donatella Lorch, *Newsweek*

Donatella Lorch began covering war in 1988 as a free-lancer in Pakistan and Afghanistan. She later worked as a broadcaster (NBC News) and print reporter (The New York Times) in the Persian Gulf, Somalia and Kosovo. She currently covers the justice system for Newsweek.

"As a young man, you feel you're not going to get hit, and I think that's the tragedy of what happens to a great many young men, both soldiers and journalists and others. I had that sense of invincibility that goes with being young.

"There were times when I was afraid . . . but, you know, war, as many people have observed before, tends to be long periods of boredom interspersed with brief moments of terror, and I think that's exactly right. I no longer believe that I'm going to live forever. Back then, intellectually, I knew that I wouldn't, but viscerally, I was convinced that nothing would happen to me, and it's just through sheer luck that nothing did."

"I've walked through mine fields. I've been rocketed. I had a horrible experience in Afghanistan: We were hiding in a cave and the Soviet troops had pinpointed us and they slammed us with rockets. I was right behind the guy in the cave opening and a rocket hit him and wounded him in the chest. . . .

"I have been very scared at times. I lost, in one year, seven friends killed and there are times when it takes a long time for it to sink in; for you to realize how it has affected your life.

"Four of my friends were killed in Mogadishu. I couldn't even react for the first week but I was still crying a year later. Years after I left Africa I still have terrible nightmares. I came out of Africa and for six months there was this darkness in my soul that nothing could remove."

Propaganda vs. Professionalism

War correspondents can be heroes – but can they be patriots? The question has tormented thoughtful war correspondents for more than a century, from Crimea in the 1850s to Kosovo in 2000. Put it another way: Is the first duty of the correspondent to truth or to his country? The history of warfare suggests this is not a false antithesis. Governments, understandably, put a priority on nurturing the morale of the armed forces and the people, intimidating an enemy with the force of the national will. They have few scruples about whether they are being fair as their propaganda demonizes an alien leader or even a whole population. The enemy is doing the same to them. That is the emotion wars generate, inviting a competitive ecstasy of hate. There is a duel in vicious stereotypes in propaganda posters, illustrations and headlines; populations would be astounded if they could see how they and their leaders are portrayed by the other side. Authority resents it when a newspaper or broadcast shades the black and white. Correspondents and their editors are not much inclined or able to do that in total wars of

Marine combat correspondent Sgt. Cyril O'Brien writes a story during the battle for Guam in 1944.

45

national survival, such as World War II, where a common will has formed against an indisputable evil. But in the limited, more controversial wars of recent years, it has been possible for a correspondent to report from "the other side," from Baghdad in the Gulf War or Belgrade in the Kosovo conflict.

The technology of satellite television and satellite telephones is only the nuts and bolts of it; it is even more significant that nations at war have more recently tolerated resident alien reporters because they see them as a megaphone to world opinion. The paradox is that these independent reporters at times have been less at risk from their enemy hosts than from the wrath of their countrymen. Covering Israel's war in the Lebanon in 1982, seasoned British reporter Robert Fisk observed: "Those of us who reported the human suffering caused by Israeli air raids in Beirut were told we were anti-Semitic." In the Gulf War, CNN's Peter Arnett, reporting from Baghdad as U.S. missiles landed, was accused by members of Congress of giving "the demented dictator a propaganda mouthpiece to over 100 nations." The BBC,

Paul Watson, far right, reacts to explosions in Mogadishu, Somalia, in 1993.

for doing the same, was denounced in Parliament as "BBC Baghdad."

The value of the independent correspondent was manifest in the work of Paul Watson, reporting for the *Los Angeles Times*. His Canadian passport enabled Watson to survive the expulsions in Kosovo and he operated throughout the conflict, free of censors, though not of danger from Serbian gunmen, KLA snipers and NATO bombs. This is what he had to say about listening on satellite TV to the voice of Jamie Shea, the alliance spokesman at the daily briefings in Brussels:

> *It haunted me at the strangest time, denying things I knew to be true, insisting on others that I had seen were false. . . . The bombing replaced stereotypes with a more confounding reality: Constant fear of my own country and its allies, and festering doubts about their claim to the moral high ground. It makes no difference that the bombs and the planes and pilots are from your own country when it is dark and you are lying in bed under a canopy of jet noise, tense and waiting for the sudden howling that says the blast will come in seconds and be close.*

Watson confirmed the judgment of the BBC's John Simpson in Belgrade – much resented in NATO – that the bombing was hardening Serbian opinion behind Yugoslavia's Slobodan Milosevic. But by staying in Kosovo, Watson was able to offer impartial testimony of the terror inflicted on the people.

Atrocity stories have been debased currency in the war of words. The other side's are propaganda and should be ignored or discredited by patriotic correspondents; ours are an integral part of the cause, and should be propagated with conviction, uniting people in vengefulness for a cause higher than pedantry. Only after the conflict, the zealots' argument runs, is there time enough to sift the ashes for truth. History knows now that the Germans did not, as charged in World War I, toss Belgian babies in the air and catch them on bayonets, nor boil down German corpses for glycerin for munitions – a story invented by a British correspondent being pressed by his office for news of atrocities. The French did not, as the German press reported, routinely gouge out the eyes of captured German soldiers, or chop off their fingers for the rings on them. Iraqi soldiers invading Kuwait did not toss premature babies out of incubators, as *The Sunday Telegraph* in London, and then the *Los Angeles Times,* reported, quoting Reuters. The story was an invention of the Citizens for a Free Kuwait lobby in Washington and

Close-Up

HENRY VILLARD
(1835-1900)

Already nationally known at 25, Villard witnesses the early Civil War battle at Bull Run. Most journalists leave early, reporting a Union victory. Villard is among the few to stay and correctly report a Confederate triumph.

WINSTON CHURCHILL
(1874-1965)

The adventuresome young Churchill loves soldiering and writing. In the Sudan and South Africa's Boer War he has the best of both worlds, simultaneously serving as soldier and correspondent. He leads Britain as prime minister in World War II.

the teenage "witness" who testified to Congress was coached by the lobby's public relations company. It was only two years later that the whole thing was exposed for the fraud it was. But the myth galvanized public opinion at a critical moment on the need to go to war, as it was intended to.

The justification quoted for such propaganda is invariably that of a one-time war correspondent who cut a corner or two himself: "In wartime, truth is so precious that she should be attended by a bodyguard of lies." Winston Churchill's epigram is a fair defense of deception in military operations such as D-Day where democracy as truth is engaged in mortal combat with a genocidal tyranny, but it is a frail vehicle for supporting the restrictions and fabrications that attend every conflict. Democracy, not less than autocracy, is ill served when an administration, and its peoples, are blinded to what is really going on out there. And that has often been the case from the birth of independent reporting in the Crimea.

History is a mausoleum of errant emotions: Who is the more patriotic – the government that conceals the blunders its soldiers endure, the cruelties they may inflict, or the correspondent who exposes them so that they might be rectified? Didn't Russell in the Crimea deserve a medal, instead of suspicion, for describing how desperate the fighting men there were for medicine and clothing, leading eventually to the dispatch of Florence Nightingale? Was it not absurd that Henry Villard went in fear of his life from a mob after reporting the truth that the censored First Battle of Bull Run was not a Union victory but a rout? What good did it do the British army to deceive itself about the Boers in South Africa? Churchill, at 25, was a correspondent who carried a Mauser pistol and didn't hesitate to fire it when the Boers derailed an armored train he was on – an engagement in which he was lucky to be taken prisoner and not shot out of hand as a combatant. But even he, wearing his patriotism on his sleeve, was not heeded when he wrote about the new kind of guerrilla warfare in which "one individual Boer mounted in suitable country was worth from three to five regular soldiers."

The atmosphere in Britain was too jingoistic, nurtured by censorship and fed by a press only too willing to inflame opinion by announcing an atrocity on the flimsiest of evidence. In World War I, the same censorship, and the same perverted sense of patriotism, had a devastating effect. The men in the trenches knew that the portrayal of the war by the coddled and pliant correspondents was a travesty; the soldier, said G.H.

Mair of the *Sunday Chronicle,* had "a much larger detestation for the institution of the war correspondent than he even had for the [General] Staff."

It would be wrong to imply that on all these professional issues there is or has been unanimity of opinion among war correspondents. In the freewheeling Vietnam War, says Ward Just of *The Washington Post,* "you were your own Jesuit." Harrison Salisbury went to Hanoi and wrote a factual account of the effect of American bombing. To some – including this editor – he was fulfilling the proper role of the independent; he afforded a perspective we would not otherwise have. To others, he was aiding the enemy. Tom Wolfe, reporting from the aircraft carrier Coral Sea, wrote:

> *To the Americans who knew the air war in the north firsthand, it seemed as if the North Vietnamese were playing Mr. Harrison Salisbury of* The New York Times *like an ocarina, as if they were blowing smoke up his pipe and the finger work was just right and the song was coming forth better than they could have played it themselves.*

Just, meeting free-lancer Martha Gellhorn in Saigon in the mid-1960s, was struck by the difference between her atti-

49

tude and his. She identified with the Viet Cong as she had identified with the Loyalists in the Spanish Civil War 30 years before – and she contrived her stories that way. Robert Capa made no bones about it. His biographer Richard Whelan says he was unwilling to risk his life covering any war in which he did not love one side and hate the other. To Just, Gellhorn and Capa expressed attitudes that "seemed anachronistic in the cool world of 1967 where reporters of my generation prided themselves on a professional detachment. The compulsion was to tell it like it was, even if the way it was told was 'not helpful' to the effort."

But in the 1990s one of the most admired of foreign correspondents was Christiane Amanpour of CNN, who was so sympathetic to the sufferings of the Bosnians that refugees chanted her name as a mantra. "In this war," she says, "there was no way that a human being or a professional should be neutral. You have to put things in context. For me, objectivity does not mean treating all sides equally; it means giving all sides an equal hearing. It does not mean drawing a moral equivalent for all sides. I refuse to do that because I am going to report honestly." CNN was uneasy about this. Her editor, Ed Turner, agreed there was a place for analysis and commentary but insisted it should always be identified as such. "Her edi-

CNN's Christiane Amanpour reports amid the rubble of Bosnia in 1993.

James Nachtwey and other photojournalists work amid the violence of South Africa in 1994.

torializing," he added, "was not willful. Any good reporter caught up in a big story will occasionally go a step too far. That is why everybody needs an editor."

There are infinite gradations here. At one extreme there is Claud Cockburn, of *The Week,* who lied imaginatively in his dispatches, down to inventing one wholly fictitious battle to induce France to reopen supply routes to the Spanish Loyalists. Arthur Koestler, of the *London News Chronicle,* mixed fake and authenticated atrocity stories. Such distortion is a betrayal of journalism,

and there is no justification for it. Herbert Matthews, who was just as sympathetic to the Loyalists, made his bias clear and gave all the facts. The problem in his case was a Catholic pro-Nationalist desk at *The New York Times.* When Matthews reported the important truth that Mussolini had sent Italian soldiers to fight with Gen. Francisco Franco's Nationalists – Matthews talked to them, saw the dead Italians being buried –

51

Inside Story

HELPING OR HINDERING: THE HUMAN DIMENSION

At what point do journalists put aside professional detachment to help another human being?

Malcolm Browne

Reporter Floyd Gibbons helps a wounded Marine in World War I and loses an eye. AP's Malcolm Browne, in shock and unable to help a Vietnamese Buddhist monk who sets himself afire, numbly snaps off roll after roll of film. In Korea, journalist Alan Dower boldly holds a South Korean official at gunpoint to halt refugee executions.

Newspaper photographer Kevin Carter's story is instructive: In the Sudan in 1993 he sees a starving child crawling to a feeding center. Lurking nearby is a vulture. Carter shoots the photo, then chases away the vulture. Complying with official warnings about disease, he does not help the little girl. The photo wins the Pulitzer Prize. But memories haunt Carter, who is sharply criticized for his inaction. A little more than a year later he is dead, an apparent suicide at age 33.

There are no simple answers.

the editors in New York insisted on substituting the word "insurgent" for "Italian," even in Matthews' sentence, "they were Italian and nothing but Italian."

How far should professional detachment be carried? It is a violation of the Geneva Conventions for a reporter to participate directly in military actions. Clearly, Churchill was out of line, and so were James Creelman of the *New York Journal,* who took part in a bayonet charge in the Spanish-American battle at El Caney; photojournalist Jimmy Hine, who carried out espionage in Cuba on the eve of the Spanish-American War; and Hemingway, who made himself the de facto commander of a group of French resistance fighters in 1944 and took a tommy gun into operations against German troops.

There are harder calls in weighing professional detachment and humanitarian impulses. Was Don McCullin taking part in a military action when, in the battle for Hue in Vietnam, he carried a wounded Marine to a first aid station? In Cambodia, he made himself unpopular by giving two newly captured Khmer prisoners some chocolate and water. "None of the real world judgments seem to apply," he said, "What's peace, what's war, what's dead, what's right, what's wrong." James Nachtwey has a rough rule that when he encounters people who have

A sequence of Eddie Adams photos captures the execution of a Viet Cong prisoner in Saigon in 1968, which shocks and outrages the world. Adams is remorseful: "I destroyed [the gunman's] life. The guy was a hero."

53

Bayonet executions in Dhaka, Bangladesh, photographed by Horst Faas and Michel Laurent.

been wounded or are about to be attacked, he'll help if he is the only one who can, otherwise he does his job, which is to photograph the scene. But he has saved victims from mobs in Haiti and South Africa, "rather than stand around to make great pictures of this person getting lynched." Nachtwey says he would draw the line at carrying ammunition.

Peter Arnett had a camera with him when another Buddhist monk started to immolate himself outside the Saigon market. He recalls, "I could have prevented that immolation by rushing at him and kicking the gasoline away. As a human being, I wanted to. As a reporter I couldn't." So he took the picture. Timothy Baker, who reported the Bosnian war, has a homely justification for the photographer sticking to his trade in such circumstances. "On a farm in California I saw a dog savaging a sheep. I could have stopped it. I didn't. I took a photograph and the picture convinced the dog owner to restrain his dog – and compensate the sheep herders – so that more than one sheep was saved."

Photographers have the special dilemma that the presence of a camera may affect behavior. Television cameraman Sorius Samura cannot bear watching a street scene he filmed in 1999 in the Sierra Leone civil war of a young man pleading unsuccessfully for his life. Samura torments himself that his camera may have provoked the soldier to kill: "I still can't forgive myself." In the India-Pakistan war in 1971, a dozen or so photographers were present when Bengali soldiers dragged four Bihari prisoners before an angry mob on the Dhaka racetrack and began stabbing them with bayonets. Marc Riboud walked away in disgust.

He and others felt that their cameras were inciting the soldiers. Horst Faas and Michel Laurent stayed to photograph the bayoneting, which went on until all four prisoners were dead. One picture ran on the front page of *The New York Times,* and Faas and Laurent won the Pulitzer Prize.

When I wrote my book "Pictures on a Page" in 1972, I criticized these awards. I thought the Pulitzer committee had erred because their awards to Faas and Laurent might induce other photographers to linger in circumstances when their presence incited violence. In his 1998 book, "Get the Picture," John Morris, the photo editor of *The New York Times* at the time, told us that he, too, had been disturbed by the ethics of publishing the picture on the front page. Many years later, says Morris, Marc Riboud told him that Prime Minister Indira Gandhi said the publication of the murder photos had so shocked and embarrassed Indian authorities that severe orders had been issued to stop such incidents. "Faas and Laurent," said Morris, "performed a public service." I am an admirer of those photographers. I respect their professionalism and admire their courage. Still, I remain troubled that the Pulitzer board was, by inference, criticizing the photographers who walked away.

Pulitzer Prize-winner Kevin Carter convinced himself that he was right to photograph the first known public execution in South Africa by "necklacing," setting fire to a gasoline-filled tire around someone's neck. "I was appalled at what they were doing. I was appalled at what I was doing. But then people started talking about those pictures . . . then I felt that maybe my actions hadn't been at all bad. Being a witness to something this horrible wasn't necessarily such a bad thing to do." Carter later took his own life.

Many correspondents have responded to their humanitarian instincts. Legendary photographer Eugene Smith said his private thought was that he would use his photographs to make an indictment of war. When he was challenged that that sounded naïve and unprofessional, he responded that there were some things you had to attempt even though you knew you were going to fail. He gave a compelling example of what might be achieved by a professional with a conscience. He was preparing to photograph another Pacific landing in World War II when the Navy asked *Life* to let him photograph an American camp for Japanese who had surrendered. The idea was that the Navy would drop the magazine on other islands and on Japan itself, so that the people would see how well captives were treated and more would surrender. But Smith knew the place

Eugene Smith

and told an admiral, "It's a terrible place, a stinking hole." The admiral said he just had a report that morning that conditions were good, which provoked Smith: " 'All right,' I said, 'I'll show you your concentration camp, your stockade.' And I went out and photographed it with a great deal of anger, because there were six people dying for every one that should have. Fifteen thousand people had access to only one or two water supplies. It was a terrible mess, badly run by our own people. I brought the pictures back and the censors were furious. For once, they were angry at the pictures and not me. They took it to higher authority and the concentration camp was completely changed around."

Knightley tells the story of an even bolder intervention, by Alan Dower, who reported the Korean War for the *Melbourne Herald*. Dower, reporter Rene Cutforth and cameraman Cyril Page saw a column of women being marched off to jail; many were carrying babies. The journalists were told the families were all to be shot because someone in the street had identified them as communists. Dower, who was a commando before he was a reporter, was carrying a carbine. He bullied his way into the jail, where the trio of journalists found that the women had been made to kneel with their babies in front of an open pit, two machine guns at their backs. Dower threatened to shoot the guard unless he took the trio to the prison governor's office. There Dower aimed his carbine at the governor and threatened: "If those machine guns fire, I'll shoot you between the eyes." Dower, making another threat, that of publicity, secured a promise from the United Nations command in Seoul that it would stamp out such practices.

Did Dower break the normal limits of journalism? Yes, and he was right to do so. One's first duty is to humanity, and there are exceptional occasions when that duty overrides the canons of any profession.

PROPAGANDA VS. PROFESSIONALISM

The Gulf War: 'An object lesson'

Christiane Amanpour, *CNN*

Christiane Amanpour's reporting — much of it done from high-risk locations — has made her one of the most recognizable broadcast journalists in the world. In the past decade, CNN's chief international correspondent has filed reports from war zones in Bosnia, Haiti, Algeria, Rwanda and the Persian Gulf.

"Those of us who think back on the Gulf War coverage, we'd never do it again the way we were forced to do it then. The Pentagon and the Western military establishment simply did not want reporters fouling up their war. For [many of] them Vietnam was the paradigm: The U.S. military establishment basically blames the press for losing the war in Vietnam.

"And so behind our backs, behind the backs of the field reporters, field producers and crews on the ground, our bosses made deals with the establishment to create 'pools' – what I call ball-and-chain, handcuffed, managed news reporting.

"They said it was because of military operational security. But we reporters would never reveal things that were supposed to be war secrets or military security. What happened was news management – because of image more than because of military security. That had a very, very negative and profoundly bad effect on the coverage and subsequent war coverage and on subsequent deals in which the Pentagon has tried to snare us. It was an object lesson on how never, ever to cover a military conflict."

Christiane Amanpour, above; John Quinones.

John Quinones, *ABC*

John Quinones began his broadcast career in radio and got his first television job with the CBS affiliate in Chicago. Since 1982 he has worked for ABC. Quinones has covered conflict throughout Central America, including the U.S. invasion of Panama in 1989.

"[Panamanian dictator] Gen. Manuel Noriega was in total control of the country, a dictator in every sense of the word. He controlled so much of that country that nothing went through there without his tacit approval.

"Initially he treated us very, very well. He invited me to ride in his private plane. When I first got there, I was the only Hispanic reporter, so that gave me an in. He kind of liked the fact that I could speak to him in Spanish and interview him in Spanish and not have to worry about his translations.

"But when he found out that we were journalists at the very core, and were going to ask the tough questions that everyone else was asking, he didn't like me very much after that. He didn't invite me on his planes and after a while wouldn't even take my calls."

Secrecy vs. the Story

Alan Dower's story exemplifies the pith of the declaration by the British Ministry of Defense during the war to recapture the Falkland Islands from Argentina in 1982: "The essence of successful warfare is secrecy; the essence of successful journalism is publicity."

Therein lies the perpetual tension between authority and the war correspondent. President John F. Kennedy, after the Bay of Pigs fiasco in 1961, put it this way: "Every newspaper now asks itself with respect to every story: 'Is it news?' All I suggest is that you add the question 'Is it in the interest of national security?'" But it was Kennedy, too, who told Orvil Dryfoos, publisher of *The New York Times*, that if the newspaper had played up the projected invasion, it might have saved him from making a terrible mistake.

Conceivably, America might have been saved from an even more terrible mistake if the newspapers had been privy at the time to the deliberations of Presidents Kennedy and Lyndon B. Johnson over Indochina. That

Allied war correspondents at the press center in Paris, 1918.

GERMAN
WAR PRACTICES

ISSUED BY
THE COMMITTEE ON PUBLIC INFORMATION
THE SECRETARY OF STATE
THE SECRETARY OF WAR
THE SECRETARY OF THE NAVY
GEORGE CREEL

Edition of January, 1918

Propaganda booklet produced by the Committee on Public Information in World War I.

story did not emerge until 1971, when Daniel Ellsberg gave Neil Sheehan of *The New York Times* 7,000 pages of secret government documents, the record of how three succeeding presidents, lacking in candor, took the country step by step into the quagmire. Arthur Ochs Sulzberger, by then the publisher of the *Times,* took a considerable risk in deciding to publish the "Pentagon Papers," as the documents came to be called, and in fighting the restraining orders secured by President Richard Nixon. The case is often misunderstood. Nixon was not defending his own policies in Vietnam. The papers were about preceding Democratic administrations. Nixon was arguing Kennedy's case for national security on policy-making. The Supreme Court's 6-3 ruling in favor of publication gloriously endorsed the people's right to know. Earlier, U.S. District Court Judge Murray Gurfein had vindicated the role of the war correspondent when he declared: "The security of the nation is not at the ramparts alone. Security also lies in the value of our free institutions."

The relationship of journalism to government is complex, one of dependence and antagonism. Without the cooperation of the armed services, which controlled access and communications, the American press could not have hoped to cover Vietnam. The British press had even less hope that it could cover Britain's attempt to repossess small islands in a battle zone 8,000 miles from London. Yet without a sympathetic press, the British government could not hope to sustain support at home for an apparently insurmountable task, and win the propaganda war.

The Persian Gulf War, in 1991, offered the same exchange, a measure of access in return for a measure of official control. In both the Falklands and the gulf, the media fundamentally supported armed intervention but complained furiously about the restrictions on what they could report. Of the restrictions, former CBS anchor Walter Cronkite protested: "What are they trying to hide?" British reporter Robert Fisk argued for "rational censorship," but on the condition that the press "should be free to go where it wants when it wants, to see, hear and photograph in the public interest." Gen. Colin Powell rebutted the press complaints: "The image of World War II's legendary Ernie Pyle, filing stories from European foxholes and Pacific beachheads, was thrown in our faces by our critics. Yet, press coverage of Desert Storm was unprecedented. Of the 2,500 scheduled journalists overall, 1,400 crowded the theater of operations at the peak. Compare this figure with 27 reporters going ashore with the first wave at Normandy on D-Day." For all the complaints, said Powell, the gulf correspondents had much more freedom than their predecessors: "Of the 1,350 print stories submitted by press pool reporters, *one* was changed to protect intelligence procedures."

In the 1982 Falklands war, the precursor for Gulf War procedures, the compromise between publicity and security was to give berths on Royal Navy ships to 29 correspondents, and to have at least one civilian information officer to act as liaison between the military and the press. The "minders," as the intermediaries came to be called, had a thankless task. There was a total lack of knowledge and sympathy between the military and the media. The journalists thought the navy obstructive and the minders ineffectual. Both in the South Atlantic and in London, censorship sometimes imposed unnecessary delays and made crass deletions for tone and taste. After the shooting was over, the press was angry to discover it had been used to feed misinformation to the enemy. ("We did not tell a lie – but we did not tell the whole truth," was the official gloss.)

The Royal Navy, for its part, found the journalists arrogant and intemperate. Correspondents with the task force heading to the Falklands became angry when they were not allowed to report that helicopter operations had been grounded by fog. It seemed absurd for the weather to be "classified." On that particular day, as it happens, the fog was confined to barely 40 miles of the South Atlantic, a fact that would be known to Argentinean defenders. Reporting the grounding would have given away the position of the task force, rendering it vulnerable to attack by Argentina's submarines. The navy protested that a *Sunday Times* reference to influenza in Port Stanley implicitly revealed Britain's ability to read enemy radio traffic. The newspaper had never thought of that point and promised to blur things in the future.

The history of war reporting suggests that correspondents and editors do not willfully betray operational secrets. Peter Preston, the editor of *The Guardian,* spoke for the industry when he advised his reporters that there would be no bonuses for producing a scoop that got somebody killed. "It is not necessarily a question of patriotism, it is a sense of realism that you don't want to put the lives of your fellow countrymen at risk." Still less do reporters want to put their own lives at risk. The responsibility of the Falklands correspondents increased, an officer noted, in direct proportion to the danger to which they were exposed. Overseeing

U.S. Secretary of Defense Dick Cheney, left, and Chairman of the Joint Chiefs of Staff Colin Powell at a Pentagon briefing during the 1989 invasion of Panama.

America's invasion of Panama, Gen. Powell became angry with bureau chiefs and network executives in New York who whined that their correspondents were in danger in the Marriott Hotel and should be rescued. Powell said no. They were safe and there were 35,000 other Americans he had to worry about. But the press pressure got to be too much for Defense Secretary Dick Cheney, who ordered Powell to go to the "rescue." The 82nd Airborne Division took casualties doing this errand. Three GIs were wounded – one seriously – and a Spanish photographer was killed by American fire. Powell asked that national security adviser Brent Scowcroft stop these orders from the sidelines just because of press flak. "We could not, in a country pledged to free expression," Powell later wrote, "simply turn off the press. But we were going to have to find a way to live with this unprecedented situation."

I believe relationships between untutored media and suspicious military are likely to get worse, largely for generational reasons. A postwar study of the Falklands conflict by British journalists Derrik Mercer, Geoff Mungham and Kevin Williams concluded that the journalists' troublesome ignorance of military affairs in general, and the Royal Navy in particular, was characteristic of a generation that had not served any time in

Inside Story

IDIOSYNCRASIES CAN SHORT-CIRCUIT THE NEWS

Sometimes, even the best reporting doesn't make a difference.

Sulzberger, above, and McCormick.

Before America enters World War II, *Chicago Tribune* publisher Robert McCormick gets letters from his Berlin bureau chief, Sigrid Schultz, warning that large numbers of Jews and others are being enslaved and executed. World War I veteran McCormick, an isolationist, fears that such "sensational" stories will help propel the nation into Europe's war. He ignores Schultz.

On the East Coast, *New York Times* publisher Arthur Hayes Sulzberger, who is Jewish, worries that if he gives extensive, front-page coverage to the murder of Jews, people will regard the newspaper as a Jewish publication. He downplays such stories, burying most on inside pages. Other newspapers, following the *Times'* lead, give such stories similar treatment.

Because of publishers' fears, two of the most prestigious newspapers in the country fail to adequately report one of the biggest stories of World War II – the Holocaust.

63

the military, unlike correspondents in earlier wars. The Persian Gulf War in 1991 witnessed a similar phenomenon: many of the younger reporters had little experience covering the military; most had never worn their country's uniform. In the Suez War of 1956, the reporters with the fleet and the editors at home had either served in World War II or been postwar conscripts; the World War II reporters were of the same generation as the military men and identified easily with them.

Two other factors will increase the likelihood of tension. Limited wars are so short there is no time for mutual trust to develop. Ernie Pyle captured the difference between then and now when he wrote to his wife in 1945 explaining why he had to go to the Pacific, having survived the war in Europe. "I've been part of the misery and tragedy of it for so long . . . I feel if I left it, it would be like a soldier deserting."

Secondly, that older generation of war correspondents had recent memory or personal experience of disasters from careless reporting.

The classic blunder of inadvertence making the case for censorship occurred in 1942 when the *Chicago Tribune* reported the Battle of Midway in a way that could have prolonged the war with Japan. The story has been much garbled over 50 years, so it is worth setting the record right, with acknowledgements to the interviews by Richard Norton Smith for his 1997 biography of *Tribune* publisher Robert McCormick ("The Colonel"). One of the closest kept secrets of World War II was that the U.S. Navy had broken much of the Japanese naval code. It was foreknowledge of the Japanese fleet movements that enabled Adm. Chester Nimitz to ignore a feint and concentrate his carriers near Midway to win a decisive victory.

No American correspondents were at Midway, but a colorful *Tribune* reporter, Stanley Johnston, was with the carrier Lexington when it was sunk in the preceding Battle of the Coral Sea. Johnston was a giant Australian, a champion sculler and a World War I hero. He had been recommended for a Victoria Cross for his valor at Gallipoli and in France. When the Lexington was hit, he made heroic efforts to rescue badly burned sailors from the ship's hold. He was very popular when transferred to another ship for transport back to the United States, and spent much of the time in the quarters occupied by the Lexington's executive officer, Cmdr. Mort Seligman.

Johnston, writing his account of Coral Sea while in Seligman's cabin, noticed a blue-lined paper that had the names of Japanese warships in an order of battle. He copied the list and later took this "dope" with him into the *Tribune* offices. His editor, Pat Maloney, was interested mainly in the Coral Sea account, but he accepted a sidebar on the Japanese order of battle at Midway, which Johnston hurriedly wrote. Johnston wouldn't reveal his source, but assured Maloney he had checked the list against "Jane's Fighting Ships." Maloney rewrote the first two "muddy" paragraphs, then wrote a headline that was not justified by Johnston's text:

NAVY HAD WORD OF JAP PLAN TO STRIKE AT SEA
KNEW DUTCH HARBOR WAS A FEINT

Maloney did not clear the story with censors, convincing himself that there was nothing in the guidelines to suppress news about the movement of hostile ships. And then, to protect Johnston's real source, Maloney attributed the story to "reliable sources in naval intelligence" and put on it a fake Washington, D.C., dateline.

The Navy was appalled. The Japanese had only to read the *Tribune* to realize that such knowledge could only mean that their codes had been compromised. President Franklin D. Roosevelt – a bitter enemy of McCormick – initially was disposed toward sending Marines in to shut down Tribune Tower. He was talked out of that, then considered trying McCormick for treason, which carried a death penalty in wartime. It ended up with the attorney general taking the *Tribune* men to a

Stanley Johnston's story (center of page) could have tipped Japan that U.S. forces had broken its military codes.

Close-Up

KEITH MURDOCH
(1886-1952)

In World War I, the Australian newsman helps make public the British military debacle at Gallipoli, Turkey. Upon returning to Australia he starts the media company that his son, Rupert Murdoch, develops into an international conglomerate.

WILLIAM HOWARD RUSSELL
(1820-1907)

In the Crimean War, Russell's reports of an ill-fed and ill-equipped British army help bring down the government. He is among the first to report a war as an independent, civilian correspondent.

grand jury. But there was no cooperation from the Navy, which rightly was concerned that a trial would mean disclosing the code-breaking. The grand jury refused to indict. The Japanese missed the *Tribune* blunder – as they also missed the false charge by columnist and broadcaster Walter Winchell that the *Tribune* knowingly had based its story on a decoded Japanese message.

I don't think any professional war correspondent today would intentionally betray that kind of secret, or do what Russell did in the Crimean War when he disclosed the number of English guns moved to the front, their exact positions, and that there was a shortage of round shot. Maybe he presumed the Russians were not readers of *The Times*. The Russian commander at Sebastapol, as it happened, said later that he never learned anything from *The Times* that he did not already know from his spies. But far more frequent than such journalistic excesses have been the excesses of censorship and harassment of the press – not to save the lives of men but to protect the careers of military brass and politicians. The public has no "need to know" the date and route of a troopship sailing, but it does need to know when scandals are being covered up. Reporters in Vietnam were beaten up by Ngo Dinh Diem's police thugs and television equipment was destroyed, because they exposed the corruption and incompetence of the regime. In World War I, censorship was used to conceal that American doughboys suffered because of chronic shortages of equipment, and that men returning from the front lines in the winter of 1917-18 were dying from pneumonia for want of dry clothing and warm housing. Heywood Broun returned home to the *New York World* office to reveal the equipment scandal. Thus breaking his correspondent's pledges cost him his accreditation and his paper a fine of $10,000. But censors blocked Westbrook Pegler's attempt to alert the public to the cause of the death rate from pneumonia. The commanding general, John J. Pershing, got the United Press reporter recalled from the front ostensibly because of his youth and inexperience: At 23, Pegler was the youngest correspondent at U.S. headquarters.

Many more men would have died needlessly at Gallipoli, Turkey, in World War I if

United Press reporter Frank Tremaine passes his story to a Navy censor in 1945.

an enterprising correspondent had not broken his word. Keith Murdoch was a 29-year-old Australian parliamentary reporter who wangled his way to Gallipoli on a mission to report back to the government on the postal arrangements for Australian troops. He persuaded Gen. Ian Hamilton to let him visit the battlefront where British, Australian and New Zealand troops were trapped under Turkish shellfire. He promised not to impart military information to anyone "unless first submitted to the Chief Field Censor." But while at Gallipoli he talked with Ellis Ashmead-Bartlett, an experienced war correspondent for the *Daily Telegraph,* who convinced him that the British and Australian governments had to be told that Hamilton was presiding over a disaster. Murdoch agreed to go back to London with an uncensored message from Ashmead-Bartlett. But in Marseille, British officials arrested Murdoch. He had been betrayed by *The Guardian*'s man

Australian troops on the attack shortly before the Allies' ill-fated Gallipoli campaign ends.

at Gallipoli and had to hand over the dispatch. Undeterred, Murdoch recounted all of the dispatch he could remember in a private letter to Australia's prime minister – who leaked it to British political leader David Lloyd George, a critic of the Gallipoli campaign. British Prime Minister Herbert Asquith demanded his own copy. The upshot was the dismissal of Hamilton and the evacuation of the beachhead.

Did Murdoch do the right thing? I think he did, but it is an agonizing decision for a correspondent when men are under fire and his honor is at stake. In January 1944, 50,000 American and British troops were led into near-disaster in Italy by poor generalship at Anzio. British and American correspondents thought Anzio could be a repeat of the Allied escape from Dunkirk in 1940. Did the public have a right to know? Prime Minister Winston Churchill thought not. He ordered the closure of radio transmitters and, in addition to security censorship, a blackout on discussions of military policy. Correspondents and newspapers in both countries protested. But there were cheers in the House of Commons when Churchill defended his suppressions: "Such words as 'desperate' ought not to be used about the position in a battle of this kind when they are false. Still less should they be used if they were true.

SECRECY vs. THE STORY

'I was just there to report'

Paul Green,
The Stars and Stripes

Paul Green got his first reporting job in July 1941 and was drafted into the Army a year later. He was transferred to the staff of The Stars and Stripes in 1943. As an "S&S" correspondent he covered World War II action in Sicily, Italy, France, Germany and elsewhere.

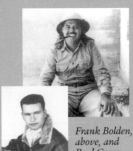

Frank Bolden,
above, and
Paul Green.

Frank Bolden,
The Pittsburgh Courier

Frank Bolden covered World War II for The Pittsburgh Courier, a newspaper with a predominantly black readership. He interviewed some of the most powerful men in the world at the time — Stalin, Churchill and Roosevelt among them — and also reported on black GIs serving in Burma and Europe.

"The soldiers who put out the paper actually controlled the paper. But let's not forget that every single line that was printed in any edition on any page was subject to military censorship. But the military censorship then – which is not true of our later wars – was restricted to military matters.

"You couldn't, of course, give any idea of coming actions. You couldn't give any designations of military units. You always said, 'A division.' Well, of course, after a while many of those numbers were released, but until then, you could not use those means of identification.

"And they kept to that. During the war there was almost no effort – occasionally here and there some wise-guy officer tried to mix into it – but basically there was no censorship on the basis of what the American public had to know and was entitled to know. So it was very good that way.

"Reporters never saw actually true action in Iraq. They always were told what had happened. There was none of that in World War II and we were very proud of that."

"The War Department realized that I wasn't there to fight the race problem. I was just there to report on what the black troops were doing [in World War II].

"When I got overseas and had to have my dispatches pass through three censorships – the Americans, the Russians and the British – I always took my dispatches to the British and the Russians first, and the Americans third. Because if the first two passed the stories, the American censor would be afraid or ashamed to countermand them. That's how I got stories on discrimination out.

"Everyone knew that the Army and Navy were segregated; I didn't dwell on that. I dwelt on what the men were doing. Back home, the people want to know, 'What's my friend or my son doing?' My whole job was to report on what they were doing. I also reported on how the soldiers and sailors were treated and mistreated. I feel that the censors would never have let my dispatches get through on the mistreatment, if on the other hand, I wasn't pointing out the good things those young men were doing."

First Draft vs. Final View

Truth! It was the isolationist senator from California, Hiram Johnson, who coined the epigram, "The first casualty when war comes is truth." It is an elusive value in the best of circumstances. In war it is a hostage to chaos and to uncontrollable passions and prejudices – "the spirit of ruthless brutality" that President Woodrow Wilson said war releases even among civilized men.

A well-informed war correspondent of integrity, writing talent and good judgment may be on the spot, and trying to tell a straight story, in its context, but, as well as official obfuscation, such a "first rough draft of history" has to survive the preconceptions of editors and competitive jealousies. Four big stories serve to illustrate what good correspondents may be up against as well as bullets: the Russian civil war ending in the Bolshevik Revolution, the Holocaust, the atomic bomb and Vietnam.

Marine correspondents (from left) Bob Cooke and Dan Levin work at a makeshift press center on the volcanic sands of Iwo Jima in February 1945.

71

Frazier Hunt of the Chicago Tribune, *right, talks to officers in France in 1918.*

Russia: Only a handful of correspondents and newspapers emerge with credit in reporting the overthrow of the czar, the violent civil war and the intervention by Allied troops against the triumphant Bolsheviks. Too many newspapers did not tell the public what was happening, but what newspaper editors and political leaders fervently wished were so – that in 1917 there was no danger of the Russian army deserting the cause; then that the czar was safe; then that Bolshevism would soon perish. The Allied intervention war was so underreported that even today many Americans do not know that 5,000 Polish-Americans from Michigan and Wisconsin joined British forces in Archangel, while 7,000 others went to Siberia to link up with Japanese troops in an attempt to smash the revolution.

In an article for *The New Republic* in 1920, Walter Lippmann and Charles Merz examined coverage of the Russian Revolution in what was by then the country's greatest newspaper, *The New York Times,* and concluded it was "nothing short of a disaster." According to Lippmann and Mertz, "the news columns were profoundly and crassly influenced by the hopes of the men who ran the paper. On the essential questions, the net effect was almost always misleading." Between November 1917 and November 1919, the *Times* reported on no fewer than 91 occasions that the Bolshevik regime was on the verge of collapse. Official censorship was not to blame. "The chief censor and the chief propagandist were hope and fear in the minds of reporters and editors." Their contribution to public understanding at a time of supreme crisis "was about as useful as that of an astrologer or alchemist." The same criticism could be made of the statesmen – including Woodrow Wilson – the military missions, the diplomats and much of the press around the world, including London's *Times.* But a rough draft of history did emerge from the bravery and independence of four journalists – John Reed of *The Masses,* Morgan Phillips Price of *The Guardian,* Arthur Ransome of Britain's *Daily News* and Frazier "Spike" Hunt of the *Chicago Tribune.*

The work by the colorful Hunt, who was alone in predicting that the Bolshevik Reds would win, is a brilliant exception to the time. He horse-sledded almost 1,000 miles from Archangel up frozen rivers and snowbound forests to reach American outposts, then sneaked out a 5,000-word cable via Norway that helped to have the isolated U.S. troops recalled from a foolish mission. Then he traveled in an armored train with the Siberian peasant Red soldiers and learned

John Reed in 1915.

enough to predict that the Bolsheviks would win. The crowning achievement, though, was John Reed's. He was passionately on the side of the Bolsheviks, attended their riotous, marathon meetings, ate with them, slept with them and argued with them in the wild and menacing confusions in Petrograd. But he was too great an artist and reporter to pump out propaganda. Here is Reed going into a soldiers' and workers' meeting in Smolny Palace in 1917:

> *It was cold and at the outer gate the Red Guards had built themselves a bonfire. At the inner gate, too, there was a blaze, by the light of which the sentries slowly spelled out our passes and looked us up and down. The canvas covers had been taken off four rapid-fire guns on each side of the doorway, and the ammunition-belts hung snake-like from their breeches. The long, bare, dimly illuminated halls roared with the thunder of feet, calling, shouting.... There was an atmosphere of recklessness.*

Reed's "Ten Days That Shook the World" remains a masterpiece of reporting for vivid portraits and insights. He sees Lenin as "a short stocky figure, bald and bulging, a leader purely by virtue of intellect; colorless, humorless, uncompromising and detached, without picturesque idiosyncrasies, but with the power of explaining profound ideas in simple terms." He sees Leon Trotsky "standing up with a pale, cruel face, letting out his rich voice in cool contempt." He is prophetic: "In the relations of a weak government with a rebellious people there comes a time when every act of the authorities exasperates the masses, and every refusal to act excites their contempt." He saw it happen.

And yet Reed was a pariah. His anti-war views and radical politics made him suspect in the eyes of U.S. authorities. His writings in the left-wing *Masses* twice led to trials on charges of sedition. Although acquitted on both occasions, when he returned to the United States from Petrograd his papers were seized and held by the government for more than a year.

The Holocaust: Sigrid Schultz was not a fine writer like Reed, but she was a superb news-gatherer. On Aug. 23, 1939, the world was in what *Time* called a state of "stunned surprise" when Adolf Hitler and Josef Stalin signed a nonaggression treaty; Shultz wasn't. As Berlin bureau chief for the *Chicago Tribune,* she had learned the identity of an astrologer Hitler sometimes consulted. She interviewed the astrologer, discovered that Hitler was speaking cordially about Stalin

and surmised correctly that Hitler was seeking a rapprochement in order to further his larger plans for conquest in Europe. Her story had run on July 13 and attracted virtually no attention. In 1940 she divined a bigger truth, that Hitler had begun murdering Jews and building concentration camps. *Tribune* publisher Robert McCormick, a staunch isolationist, believed such sensational stories could propel the United States into the war. Schultz's story never ran.

The atomic bomb: At the end of World War II, after two atomic bombs had been dropped, Gen. Douglas MacArthur placed southern Japan off limits, which meant that the press was not allowed to visit Hiroshima and Nagasaki. *London Daily Express* reporter Wilfred Burchett, an Australian with strong left-wing views, managed to get to Hiroshima on a Japanese train. What he saw gave the lie to the official accounts. He noted that a month after the bombing, people who were unhurt at the time were dying of what he called "the atomic plague." That, of course, was radiation sickness. U.S. authorities denied there was any such thing and accused Burchett of being influenced by Japanese propaganda.

During the development of the atomic bomb, project director Gen. Leslie Groves secretly hired William L. Laurence, a highly

John Hersey in Europe in 1944; first page of his New Yorker article, 1946.

respected science reporter with *The New York Times,* to act as the project's official historian. Laurence eagerly accepted the job – his scientific curiosity and patriotic zeal perhaps blinding him to the notion that he was at the same time compromising his journalistic independence. After the bombing, the brilliant but bullying Groves continually suppressed or distorted the effects of radiation. He dismissed reports of Japanese deaths as "hoax or propaganda." The *Times'* Laurence weighed in, too, after Burchett's reports, and parroted the government line.

It was left to John Hersey to bring the truth to light in a way that could not be denied. Born in China, son of American missionaries, Hersey covered the war in Europe and the Pacific. He was assigned by *The New Yorker* magazine to write about what happened at Hiroshima. He decided to model his report on Thornton Wilder's "The Bridge of San Luis Rey," dramatizing the significance of the bomb for mankind by the stories of six survivors from exactly 8:15 a.m. on Aug. 6, 1945. Hersey's 1946 account raised reporting to the level of literature and created waves that still ripple. "Hiroshima," like "Ten Days That Shook the World," is a classic of journalism that lives beyond its headlines.

Vietnam: This was not the first uncensored war. But it was the most open war. The South Vietnamese regime was restrictive, but the U.S. government allowed reporters to move freely in combat zones and took them there in military transport. It did this even for foreign reporters known to be hostile. Correspondents accredited to U.S. forces agreed to refrain from disclosing 15 categories of information (troop movement, casualties and the like) but their dispatches did not require military vetting. Gens. William Westmoreland and Winant Sidle have testified that the system worked well. Hundreds of reporters went to Vietnam, but from 1966 onward, accreditation was withdrawn only on four occasions.

The legend persists, however, that the press opposed U.S. war efforts. President Richard Nixon said the war "was the first in our history during which our media were more friendly to our enemies than our allies." Gen. Westmoreland protested that a lack of censorship leads to confusion and when you add television to that "you have an instrument that can paralyze this country."

It was not quite like that.

The trio of young war correspondents usually singled out for attack – *The New York Times'* David Halberstam, the AP's Malcolm Browne, and UPI's Neil Sheehan – were not critics of America's intervention. They were wholly committed to saving South Vietnam from the communists; their exasperation was with the regimes in Saigon, which they thought would lose the war. The correspondents cheered the battle successes; they identified with the gung-ho officers in the field; until 1967, they argued against withdrawal. Like the rest of the press corps and Washington journalists, they reported the war within the framework of Cold War ideology rather than nationalist revolution. So did television. What disquieted them at first, and then maddened them, were the little deceptions of the U.S. government, the hubris of its generals and the corrupt incompetence of the South Vietnamese establishment. John Mecklin, the U.S. official in charge of press relations in the early years, has written that U.S. information policy was "a long and sorry tale of deception and sometimes arrogance" and the worst feature of it was that the political-military bureaucracy deceived itself into "telling headquarters what it wants to hear." The correspondents did a real service here.

There are legitimate criticisms of the performance of the war correspondents and their sponsoring news organizations. There was too little analysis; like the administration, they did not understand the difference

77

between the insurgency in Malaya and Vietnam, differences in social and ethnic structure that doomed the "Strategic Hamlets" relocation programs on which so much ink – and blood – was spilled. They did not question President Kennedy's artful dodges. They did not expose President Johnson's evasions and subterfuges; stenographic, not investigative, energies were brought to the coverage of the crucial Gulf of Tonkin incident, LBJ's erroneous justification for a wider war. But the press cannot be indicted for lack of patriotism or empathy with the grunts. Until 1968, the editorials in *The Washington Post* were so supportive that LBJ said they were worth 50 divisions. Daniel C. Hallin ("The 'Uncensored War' "), who made an exhaustive study of press performance, writes: "In the early years before the Tet offensive and the subsequent shift in American policy from escalation to de-escalation, most news coverage was highly supportive of American intervention . . . and despite occasional crises, Kennedy and Johnson were usually able to 'manage' the news very effectively." Even in the later Nixon years, coverage was "not nearly so consistently negative as the conventional wisdom now seems to hold." Reporters continued to be patriots in the sense of portraying the Americans as "the good guys."

The chasm that opened between government and press was a crack in the ground in 1961. William Prochnau ("Once Upon a Distant War") described the world the journalists inhabited – where wounded men were denied Purple Hearts because America was not at war; where the U.S. napalm strikes they saw had not happened because Washington had said the flaming jelly was not being used. Stanley Karnow, on one of his periodic visits for *Time* magazine, had a drink with a military information officer at the Majestic Hotel overlooking picturesque Saigon harbor. Karnow was astounded to see an American aircraft carrier nosing its way through the junks and sampans to make delivery of 40 American helicopters lashed to its deck. "My God," said Karnow, "look at that carrier!" The officer replied: "I don't see nothing." When the story ran, the Defense Department asked for an investigation to "track the source of the leak." Karnow concluded that the efforts at secrecy were aimed more at fooling the American public than the Viet Cong guerrillas who watched everything that moved. At the battle of Ap Bac in 1963, Neil Sheehan burrowed into the mud as incoming shells exploded right where he had been a moment before; he was close enough both to the action and the chief American military

From left, David Halberstam, Malcolm Browne and Neil Sheehan in South Vietnam, 1963.

Close-Up

STANLEY KARNOW
(b. 1925)

A Pulitzer Prize-winning journalist and historian, Karnow covers Asia for *Time* and *Life* starting in 1959. He later reports for *The Washington Post* and other publications and writes one of the definitive histories of the Vietnam War.

GLORIA EMERSON
(b. 1930)

Emerson covers the Vietnam War for *The New York Times* from 1970 to 1972. An outspoken critic of U.S. intervention in Southeast Asia, she writes extensively about the war's effect on the Vietnamese people.

adviser to know how and why it was a shameful defeat for the better-armed South Vietnamese, while the generals were telling Washington of a victory.

The cracks kept widening. The correspondents became more skeptical, more critical, sometimes perhaps to exaggerate what went wrong, and high-level officials in the U.S. Embassy and military command whistled more loudly in the dark the tune that Washington wanted to hear. What Washington did not want to hear was *The New York Times'* Gloria Emerson describing the panic-stricken rout of the South Vietnamese army in Laos in March of 1971.

The correspondents had another battle – with their editors at home. Halberstam was in trouble at *The New York Times* for failing to appreciate the purity of prose the copy desk admired, then got into a scrap with the head office in the early 1960s about a six-part series in the competing *Herald Tribune* by Marguerite Higgins of World War II and Korea fame. Higgins, briefed by the commanding general in Vietnam, contradicted almost everything Halberstam had reported and the head office wanted to know, in not so many words, whether he was slanting his copy. Halberstam was right, but what saved him was President Kennedy's appeal to the *Times'* publisher to pull him out of Vietnam.

Morley Safer of CBS in Vietnam, 1965: His report infuriated President Lyndon Johnson.

The *Times* had quite good coverage of the war. *Time* magazine had the worst. It mutilated the copy of Charles Mohr to fit the notion that all was going swimmingly well. Then the autocratic managing editor, Otto Fuerbringer, ambushed the entire press corps: "The newsmen have themselves become a part of South Vietnam's confusion, [their] reporting prone to distortions. . . . In the camaraderie of the Hotel Caravelle's eighth-floor bar, they pool their convictions, information, misinformation and grievances. But the balm of such companionship has not been conducive to independent thought. Many of the correspondents seem reluctant to give splash treatment to anything that smacks of military victory. When there is defeat, the color is rich and flowing." Fuerbringer was writing propaganda, not journalism.

Television dominated the output of national news in the late '60s, reaching twice as many people. In author Michael Arlen's phrase, Vietnam was "the living-room war." There is no conclusive evidence that overall

Inside Story

WARTIME CONTROLS ON PRESS TIGHTEN, SPAWN DIRE FORECAST

Pool reporters in Saudi Arabia.

The U.S. invasion of Grenada in 1983 is not made public for 48 hours. News media protests lead to the creation of a Pentagon "pool" – a group of reporters selected to cover future operations. But in the first real test of the system, in the 1989 U.S. invasion of Panama, pool reporters are kept out of Panama until the heaviest fighting is over.

A pool system is maintained during the Persian Gulf War. Reporters' contacts with troops are minimal and monitored. News organizations, however, do not oppose the restrictions with a united front. *Harper's* publisher John R. MacArthur calls the situation a "disaster for the American press."

The news media fare little better during the 1999 NATO bombing of Serbia, says journalism historian Phillip Knightley. He predicts that in any future war, control of correspondents "will be even tighter and that in general this will be accepted by the media."

TV had a greater effect, proportionately, than any other news medium. Television was much more cautious than print, especially before the Tet offensive of 1968. Broadcast journalists were more reliant on the military for their information than the newspaper correspondents were, and while the soldiers supported the war, so did the networks. What little was presented of the anti-war case often was cast in less-than-flattering tones. A typical report began: "While Americans fight and die in Vietnam, there are those in this country who sympathize with the Viet Cong." (Peter Jennings, ABC, Oct. 22, 1965.)

But the potential power of television was demonstrated in August 1965. Morley Safer of CBS went on a routine patrol and filmed the torching of the village of Cam Ne by Marines applying Zippo lighters to thatched roofs. The Marines were telling the peasants in English to get out of the way of the fire, but they stayed at risk until Safer intervened to ask that his Vietnamese cameraman be allowed to speak to the villagers in their own language. Safer's report was forceful: "The day's operation burned down 150 houses, wounded three women, killed one baby, wounded one Marine, and netted four old men who could not answer questions put to them in English. . . .There is little doubt that American firepower can win a military victory here. But to a Vietnamese peasant whose home means a lifetime of backbreaking labor it will take more than presidential promises to convince him that we are on his side."

Safer's report was heard on CBS before it was seen; in those days it took time to ship film. The report immediately was slapped down by the Pentagon, which said a couple of houses had been burned accidentally. The arrival of the film at CBS gave the lie to that defense. It also provoked a certain anxiety among top CBS brass, but it was aired and had a big impact. An angry President Johnson telephoned Frank Stanton, the head of CBS, and said Stanton had just "shat on the American flag." But in context of the times, the Safer report was an exception. Television, until the 1968 Tet offensive, was mainly routine glosses from Saigon without analysis or commentary.

Tet changed everything. It was a military defeat for the Viet Cong; the guerrillas attacking the U.S. Embassy in Saigon did not penetrate the chancery as was erroneously and sensationally reported. But, as Hallin remarks, the coverage of Tet gave the public a more accurate view of the overall course of the war through the inaccurate view it gave of the outcome of that particular battle. The celebrated disavowal of faith shortly afterward by Walter Cronkite ("the most trusted man in America") was what the more morose opinion-formers were saying in the White House and Pentagon.

The conventional wisdom that television alarmed the public with gory images is not borne out by research. Only about 22 percent of film showed combat and that was minimal. Network policy was to avoid showing casualties or suffering. Fred Friendly of CBS attests that those policies shielded the public from the true horror. Arlen finds that even after 1968, "there was a nearly total absence on the nightly news broadcasts of any explicit reality of the war – certainly of any of the blood and gore or even pain of combat."

But it is a libel that the television crews covered the war from the Caravelle Hotel in Saigon. They did go into the bush with the troops, exposed to danger by the encumbrance of their gear. Many were wounded, and nine network employees died.

Is journalism worth dying for?

Reuters reporter Kurt Schork thought not. "War reporting is a job, is a craft – not a holy crusade. The thing is to work and not

Body armor worn by CNN's Peter Arnett in the Persian Gulf War.

get hurt. When that is no longer possible, it is time to get out." What drove Schork was not the chance of a front-page lead and certainly not the fame of a byline (many of his stories carried the agency byline). He was moved by the idea that he could document history. He was, as his friend Charles Lane wrote, a man of moral clarity, and in Bosnia, Kurdistan, Chechnya, East Timor, Kosovo and Sierre Leone, he found himself confronted by evil. He was outraged by the equivocations of the Western powers that doomed so many people in Bosnia from 1992 to 1995, but he did not merely vent. He channeled his anger into the pursuit of more facts, more documentation of atrocity, more first drafts of history. But he took more risks than he was willing to acknowledge.

In the spring of 2000, when Schork arrived in Sierra Leone, 12 reporters – 11 of them nationals – had died in a civil war. He teamed up with another idealist believer, Associated Press cameraman Miguel Gil Moreno de Mora. Schork had abandoned a career as a corporate lawyer because he believed it was his destiny to portray the sufferings of innocent people trapped in war. On May 24, Moreno and Schork were driving on a lonely road when they were murdered in a rebel ambush. They were the 13th and 14th correspondents to die in a stupid little war.

Is journalism worth dying for?

Is history worth dying for?

Schork and Moreno had made little contribution to the news from Sierra Leone, even less to its wretched history. Their deaths served neither history nor journalism. But their lives did more than that. They were remarkably dedicated to truth and to common humanity, as were the lives of many of the correspondents who died before them. They served their ideals with a skill and courage that will be an inspiration to all who follow their professional paths – now, I think, to all of us who so easily forget the sacrifices that may lie behind the headlines.

FIRST DRAFT vs. FINAL VIEW

'Adventures for several lifetimes'

Peter Arnett, *CNN*

Peter Arnett has covered dozens of wars in 30-plus years as a journalist. He spent more than a decade in Vietnam for The Associated Press, where he won the Pulitzer Prize in 1966. In 1991, his live reports from Baghdad for CNN were both praised and damned.

James Nachtwey, above, and Peter Arnett.

"In Vietnam, the reporters, including me, missed the story of the young GIs, the enlisted men, and the difficulties they would face after the war. That was something the press did not pick up on at all. It's a pity because we would be much more understanding of veterans if we had written about them.

"The reason we didn't was that the reporters who covered Vietnam identified with the officer corps, the West Point graduates and the older soldiers. They could tell us information on the record. They knew what was happening in the battlefield. The GIs, we tended to ignore. Occasionally, we'd write stories about their conduct. But basically, rarely interviewed them. We did not really pick up on the tremendous dislocation that these young soldiers would have with American society. And that is a pity."

James Nachtwey, *Magnum*

James Nachtwey got his first overseas photo assignment from Black Star, which sent him to Northern Ireland in 1981 to cover the turmoil there. Over the next 20 years, he photographed conflicts on every continent in countless countries.

"There was a situation in 1984 in El Salvador where once I actually turned away from making a picture. What I was witnessing was so horrible to me that I couldn't take [a photo]. That was a mistake. I came to my senses . . . and I made the picture. When I edited this roll of film, I literally jumped out of my chair when I came across that image. And I realized that it wasn't up to me to censor myself. . . . Since then I've never turned away. There's an oft-told tale of World War II where some of the photographers who entered the concentration camps were so horrified that they walked away without taking pictures. What would we do today [if no one had taken] those pictures? . . . Our own emotional well-being is one of the things that sometimes has to get sacrificed in order to fulfill our duties as journalists.

"[After] 20 years I've had enough adventures for several lifetimes; I've traveled all I would ever want to travel; and yet my sense of mission is stronger than ever. And I think that the value of communication is what endures in the end."

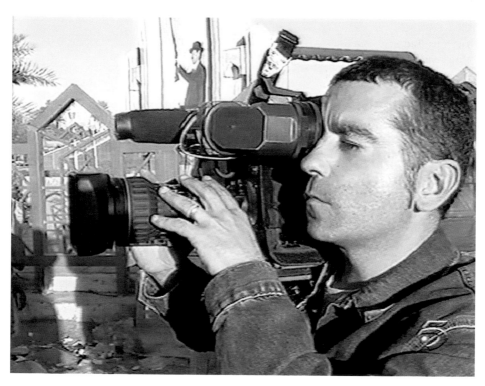

Jose Couso, a cameraman for Spain's Telecinco TV channel, films in Baghdad, Iraq, shortly before he was killed in the Palestine Hotel when it was fired on by U.S. forces. He was the second Spanish journalist killed in Iraq.

Suggested Reading

Bartimus, Tad, et al. *War Torn: Stories of War From the Women Reporters Who Covered Vietnam.* New York: Random House, 2002.

Caesar, Julius. *The Conquest of Gaul.* Translated by S.A. Handford. New York: Penguin, 1982.

Carmichael, Jane. *First World War Photographers*. London, New York: Routledge, 1989.

Churchill, Winston. *London to Ladysmith via Pretoria.* New York: W.W. Norton, 1990.

Elwood-Akers, Virginia. *Women War Correspondents in the Vietnam War, 1961-1975*. Metuchen, N.J.: Scarecrow Press, Inc., 1988.

Emery, Michael C., Edwin Emery and Nancy L. Roberts. *The Press and America: An Interpretive History of the Mass Media.* 8th ed. Needham Heights, Mass.: Allyn & Bacon, 1996.

Evans, Harold, with Gail Buckland and Kevin Baker. *The American Century.* New York: Alfred A. Knopf, Inc., 1998.

_____. *Pictures on a Page: Photo-Journalism, Graphics and Picture Editing.* New York: Holt, Rinehart and Winston, 1978.

Goff, Peter, ed. *The Kosovo News and Propaganda War.* Vienna, Austria: The International Press Institute, 1999.

Hallin, Daniel C. *The "Uncensored War": The Media and Vietnam*. Berkeley: University of California Press, 1986.

Hastings, Max. *Overlord: D-Day and the Battle for Normandy.* New York: Simon and Schuster, 1984.

Hill, Paul, and Thomas Cooper. *Dialogue With Photography.* New York: Farrar, Straus & Giroux, 1979.

Katz, Mark. *Witness to an Era: The Life and Photographs of Alexander Gardner: The Civil War, Lincoln and the West.* New York: Viking Penguin Inc., 1991.

Knightley, Phillip. *The First Casualty: The War Correspondent as Hero and Myth-Maker From the Crimea to Kosovo.* 2nd ed. London: Prion Books, Ltd., 2000.

Lebow, Arthur. *The Reporter Who Would Be King.* New York: Charles Scribner's Sons, 1992.

Library of America. *Reporting Vietnam, Part One: American Journalism, 1959-1969.* New York: Literary Classics of the United States, Inc., 1998.

_____. *Reporting Vietnam, Part Two: American Journalism, 1969-1975.* New York: Literary Classics of the United States, Inc., 1998.

_____. *Reporting World War II, Part One: American Journalism, 1938-1944.* New York: Literary Classics of the United States, Inc., 1995.

_____. *Reporting World War II, Part Two: American Journalism, 1944-1946.* New York: Literary Classics of the United States, Inc., 1995.

Loyd, Anthony. *My War Gone By, I Miss It So.* New York: Atlantic Monthly Press, 1999.

Marinovich, Greg and João Silva. *The Bang-Bang Club: Snapshots From a Hidden War.* New York: Basic Books, 2000.

McCullin, Don, with Lewis Chester. *Unreasonable Behaviour: An Autobiography.* New York: Alfred A. Knopf, 1992.

Mecklin, John. *Mission in Torment: An Intimate Account of the U.S. Role in Vietnam.* Garden City, N.Y.: Doubleday, 1965.

Mercer, Derrick, Geoff Mungham and Kevin Williams. *The Fog of War: The Media on the Battlefield.* London: Heinemann, 1987.

Morris, John G. *Get the Picture: A Personal History of Photojournalism.* New York: Random House, 1998.

Newton, Eric, ed. *Crusaders, Scoundrels, Journalists: The Newseum's Most Intriguing Newspeople.* New York: Times Books, 1999.

Perry, James M. *A Bohemian Brigade: The Civil War Correspondents, Mostly Rough, Sometimes Ready.* New York: John Wiley & Sons, 2000.

Prochnau, William W. *Once Upon a Distant War.* New York: Times Books, 1995.

Reed, John. *The Collected Works of John Reed.* New York: Modern Library, 1995.

Rollyson, Carl. *Nothing Ever Happens to the Brave: The Story of Martha Gellhorn.* New York: St. Martin's Press, 1990.

Roth, Mitchel P. *Historical Dictionary of War Journalism.* Westport, Conn.: Greenwood Press, 1997.

Smith, Richard Norton. *The Colonel: The Life and Legend of Robert R. McCormick, 1880-1955.* New York: Houghton Mifflin Co., 1997.

Sullivan, Constance, ed. *Landscapes of the Civil War: Newly Discovered Photographs From the Medford Historical Society.* New York: Alfred A. Knopf, 1995.

Tobin, James. *Ernie Pyle's War: America's Eyewitness to World War II.* New York: The Free Press, 1997.

Viola, Herman J. *Little Bighorn Remembered: The Untold Indian Story of Custer's Last Stand.* New York: Times Books, 1999.

Voss, Frederick S. *Reporting the War: The Journalistic Coverage of World War II.* Washington, D.C.: Smithsonian Institution Press for the National Portrait Gallery, 1994.

Wagner, Lila. *Women War Correspondents in World War II.* New York: Greenwood Publishing Group, Inc., 2000.

Westmoreland, William C. *"A Reply to Walter Cronkite."* Christian Science Monitor, June 7, 1982, p. 27.

Whelan, Richard. *Robert Capa: A Biography.* Lincoln, Neb.: University of Nebraska Press, 1994.

Index of Names and News Organizations

Photograph Credits

Cover photo: *James Nachtwey and other photojournalists work amid the violence of South Africa in 1994.* David C. Turnley, Corbis Images

Title page photo: *Body Armor.* (Newseum collection)

Back cover: top *Lt. Barrett Gallagher:* National Archives and Records Administration; center *Frazier Hunt:* National Archives and Records Administration; bottom *Persian Gulf grief:* David C. Turnley, Corbis Images

pp. 6-7 *Richard Harding Davis:* National Archives and Records Administration; p. 8 *Bloody Camera:* Photo by Patrick Baz, Agence France-Presse; p. 9 *David Blundy with Ariel Sharon*: Courtesy Harold Evans; p. 9 *David Blundy*: Mark Ellidge, NI Syndication; p. 14 *David Bloom*: NBC News/AP photo; pp. 16-17 *Robert Capa*: Robert Capa, Magnum Photos; p. 18 *Red Horse drawings*: National Anthropological Archives, Smithsonian Institution; p. 19 *Mark Kellogg*: Courtesy Sandy Barnard; p. 19 *Thucydides:* Library of Congress; p. 21 *William Howard Russell:* Times Newspapers Limited; p. 21 *Russell's notebook: The Times*; p. 22 *Edward R. Murrow:* Library of Congress; p. 23 *Martha Gellhorn:* The Associated Press; p. 25 *Ernie Pyle:* National Archives and Records Administration; p. 26 *Stephen Crane:* Collection of Stanley and Mary Wertheim; p. 27 *Tom Gjelten:* Courtesy Tom Gjelten; pp. 28-29 *Lt. Barrett Gallagher:* National Archives and Records Administration; p. 30 *Lowell Thomas:* Corbis Images; p. 30 *Virginia Irwin: St. Louis Post-Dispatch*; p. 31 *Bill Mauldin:* George Rodger, National Portrait Gallery ; p. 32 *Roger Fenton:* Library of Congress; p. 33 *Alexander Gardner:* Library of Congress; p. 35 *Persian Gulf grief:* David C. Turnley, Corbis Images; p. 36 *Scribners:* Library of Congress; p. 37 *Richard Harding Davis:* Courtesy Kristen Kehrig; p. 38 *Ernest Hemingway:* Courtesy John F. Kennedy Library; p. 40 *New Testament:* Courtesy Gabriel Goldberg; p. 41 *Robert Capa:* Robert Capa, Magnum Photos; p. 43 *Donatella Lorch:* Courtesy Donatella Lorch; p. 43 *Ted Koppel:* The Associated Press; pp. 44-45 *Cyril O'Brien:* Courtesy Cyril J. O'Brien; p. 46 *Paul Watson:* The Associated Press; p. 48 *Henry Villard:* Courtesy Library of the University of Oregon; p. 48 *Winston Churchill:* Hulton Getty; p. 50 *Christiane Amanpour:* CNN photo, courtesy David Rust; p. 51 *James*

Nachtwey: David C. Turnley, Corbis Images; p. 52 *Malcolm Browne:* Courtesy Malcolm Browne; p. 53 *Vietnamese execution:* Eddie Adams, The Associated Press; p. 54 *Bayonet execution:* Horst Faas/Michel Laurent, The Associated Press; p. 56 *W. Eugene Smith:* W. Eugene Smith Archive, Center for Creative Photography, University of Arizona; p. 57 *Christiane Amanpour:* Corbis/Sygma; p. 57 *John Quinones:* ABC News; pp. 58-59 *Paris press center:* National Archives and Records Administration; p. 60 *CPI booklet:* Newseum collection; p. 62 *Press conference:* Bob Pearson, Agence France-Presse; p. 63 *Arthur Hayes Sulzberger:* The Associated Press; p. 63 *Robert R. McCormick:* Colonel Robert R. McCormick Research Center; p. 65 **Chicago Sunday Tribune:** Newseum collection; p. 66 *Keith Murdoch:* The National Library of Australia; p. 66 *William Howard Russell:* Library of Congress; p. 67 *Censor at work:* National Archives and Records Administration; p. 68 *Gallipoli attack:* Corbis Images; p. 69 *Frank Bolden:* Courtesy Frank Bolden; p. 69 *Paul Green:* Courtesy Paul Green; pp. 70-71 *Marine correspondents:* National Archives and Records Administration; p. 72 *Frazier Hunt:* National Archives and Records Administration; p. 74 *John Reed:* Houghton Library, Harvard University; p. 76 *John Hersey:* The Associated Press; p. 76 *The New Yorker:* Newseum collection; p. 79 *Malcolm Browne:* The Associated Press; p. 80 *Stanley Karnow:* John Launois, Black Star, TimePix; p. 80 *Gloria Emerson:* New York Times Pictures; p. 81 *Morley Safer:* The Associated Press; p.82 , *Pool reporters:* PictureQuest, Kenneth Jarecke, Contact Press Images; p. 84 *Body armor:* Newseum collection; p. 85 *James Nachtwey:* Christopher Morris, Black Star; p. 85 *Peter Arnett:* Courtesy Peter Arnett; p. 86 *Jose Couso:* EFE, Telecinco/AP.